First World War
and Army of Occupation
War Diary
France, Belgium and Germany

33 DIVISION
19 Infantry Brigade
Cameronians (Scottish Rifles)
1st Battalion
1 December 1915 - 24 May 1919

WO95/2422/2

The Naval & Military Press Ltd
www.nmarchive.com
Published in association with The National Archives

Published by

The Naval & Military Press Ltd

Unit 10 Ridgewood Industrial Park,

Uckfield, East Sussex,

TN22 5QE England

Tel: +44 (0) 1825 749494

www.naval-military-press.com

www.nmarchive.com

This diary has been reprinted in facsimile from the original. Any imperfections are inevitably reproduced and the quality may fall short of modern type and cartographic standards.

© **Crown Copyright**
Images reproduced by permission of The National Archives, London, England, 2015.

Contents

Document type	Place/Title	Date From	Date To
Miscellaneous	WO95/2422/2 1 Bn Cameronians (R. Scottish Rifles) Dec 1915-May 1919		
Heading	83rd Division 19th Infy Bde 1st Bn Scottish Rifles (Cameronians) Dec 1915-May 1919 From 2 Div 19 Bde		
Heading	19th Inf Bde 1/Scottish Rifles Dec Vol XVII		
War Diary	Trenches Centin Scot N of Canal	01/12/1915	05/12/1915
War Diary	Billets Quesnoy	06/12/1915	07/12/1915
War Diary	Billets SE Quesuoy	08/12/1915	09/12/1915
War Diary	Billets Hamenartois	10/12/1915	26/12/1915
War Diary	Billets Hamenstion Annezin	27/12/1915	27/12/1915
War Diary	Billets Annequin	28/12/1915	28/12/1915
War Diary	Trenches	29/12/1915	04/01/1916
War Diary	Billets Annequin	05/01/1916	07/01/1916
War Diary	Bethune	08/01/1916	13/01/1916
War Diary	Trenches Cuinchy (A.2).	14/01/1916	20/01/1916
War Diary	Annequin (North)	21/01/1916	31/01/1916
Heading	1 Scottish Rifles Vol XVIII XIX		
War Diary	Billets Bethune	01/02/1916	05/02/1916
War Diary	Trenches Z 1 Cambrin	06/02/1916	18/02/1916
War Diary	Billets Annequin (South)	19/02/1916	21/02/1916
War Diary	Billets Oblinghem	21/02/1916	29/02/1916
War Diary	Annequin North	01/02/1916	02/02/1916
Miscellaneous			
War Diary	Trenches Cuinchy A2	03/03/1916	06/03/1916
War Diary	Billets Annequin (North)	07/03/1916	11/03/1916
War Diary	Trenches Cuinchy Left Subsection	12/03/1916	14/03/1916
War Diary	Billets Annequin North	15/03/1916	16/03/1916
War Diary	Oblinghem	17/03/1916	19/03/1916
War Diary	Billets Oblinghem	20/03/1916	23/03/1916
War Diary	Beuvry	24/03/1916	24/03/1916
War Diary	Trenches Auchy Left Sub-Section	25/03/1916	29/03/1916
War Diary	Billets Deuvry	30/03/1916	02/04/1916
War Diary	Trenches Auchy Left Sub-Section	03/04/1916	06/04/1916
War Diary	Billets Beuvry	07/04/1916	09/04/1916
War Diary	Bethune	10/04/1916	12/04/1916
War Diary	Billets Bethune	13/04/1916	18/04/1916
War Diary	Trenches Cuinchy Left Subsec	19/04/1916	20/04/1916
War Diary	Cuinchy Left Senlsic	20/04/1916	21/04/1916
War Diary	Trenches Cuinchy And Left Subsection	21/04/1916	22/04/1916
War Diary	Billets Le Quesnoy	23/04/1916	26/04/1916
War Diary	Trenches Cuinchy Left Sub Section	27/04/1916	30/04/1916
War Diary	Billets Le Quesnoy	01/05/1916	04/05/1916
War Diary	Billets Annezin	05/05/1916	16/05/1916
War Diary	Billets Annequin South	17/05/1916	22/05/1916
War Diary	Trenches Auchy Left And Sec	23/05/1916	27/05/1916
War Diary	Billets Annequin South	28/05/1916	31/05/1916
Heading	D.A.G. General Headquarters. 3rd Echelon. Base.		
War Diary	Billets Beuvry	01/06/1916	02/06/1916
War Diary	Trenches Auchy-Left	03/06/1916	09/06/1916
War Diary	Billets Annezin	10/06/1916	17/06/1916

War Diary	Billets Le Quesnoy	18/06/1916	19/06/1916
War Diary	Village Line Givenchy	20/06/1916	25/06/1916
War Diary	Trenches Right Sector Givenchy	26/06/1916	30/06/1916
Heading	19th Inf. Bde. 33rd Div. 1st Battn. The Cameronians (Scottish Rifles). July 1916		
War Diary	Right Section Givenchy	01/07/1916	02/07/1916
War Diary	Village Line	03/07/1916	05/07/1916
War Diary	Le Preol	06/07/1916	07/07/1916
War Diary	Oblinghem	08/07/1916	08/07/1916
War Diary	Coulainville	09/07/1916	10/07/1916
War Diary	Daours	11/07/1916	11/07/1916
War Diary	Buire	12/07/1916	13/07/1916
War Diary	Meaulte	14/07/1916	14/07/1916
War Diary	Mametz Wood	15/07/1916	15/07/1916
War Diary	High Wood	16/07/1916	16/07/1916
War Diary	Bazentin	17/07/1916	19/07/1916
War Diary	High Wood	20/07/1916	20/07/1916
War Diary	Mametz	21/07/1916	21/07/1916
War Diary	Buire Sur L'ancre	22/07/1916	31/07/1916
Heading	19th Brigade. 33rd Division. 1st Battalion Scottish Rifles (Cameronians) August 1916		
War Diary	Buire Sur. Ancre	01/08/1916	05/08/1916
War Diary	Near Becordel	06/08/1916	18/08/1916
War Diary	Near High Wood	19/08/1916	19/08/1916
War Diary	Bazentin Le Grand	19/08/1916	21/08/1916
War Diary	High Wood	22/08/1916	25/08/1916
War Diary	Bazentin	26/08/1916	27/08/1916
War Diary	Pommier Redoubt	28/08/1916	28/08/1916
War Diary	Fricourt Wood	29/08/1916	31/08/1916
Miscellaneous	D.A.G. (Theo. H.Q. 10th Infy Bde.) General Headquarters. 3rd Echelon Base.	30/09/1916	30/09/1916
War Diary	Molliens Au Bois	01/09/1916	01/09/1916
War Diary	Vacquerie	02/09/1916	02/09/1916
War Diary	Domesmont & ? Camp	03/09/1916	03/09/1916
War Diary	Villers & Hopital	04/09/1916	04/09/1916
War Diary	Oeuf	05/09/1916	05/09/1916
War Diary	Croisette	06/09/1916	07/09/1916
War Diary	Sericourt	08/09/1916	08/09/1916
War Diary	Le Souich	09/09/1916	09/09/1916
War Diary	Bienvillers Au-Bois	10/09/1916	11/09/1916
War Diary	Fonquevillers	12/09/1916	12/09/1916
War Diary	Z Sector Fonquevillers	13/09/1916	15/09/1916
War Diary	Pommier	16/09/1916	20/09/1916
War Diary	Fonque-Villers	21/09/1916	26/09/1916
War Diary	St Amand	27/09/1916	29/09/1916
War Diary	Lucheux	30/09/1916	30/09/1916
Miscellaneous	D.A.G. General Head Quarters. 3rd Echelon. Base.		
War Diary	Lucheux	01/10/1916	11/10/1916
War Diary	Hebuterne	11/10/1916	15/10/1916
War Diary	Bayencourt	16/10/1916	17/10/1916
War Diary	Iverney & Doullens	18/10/1916	18/10/1916
War Diary	Doullens	19/10/1916	19/10/1916
War Diary	Ville Sous Corbie	20/10/1916	23/10/1916
War Diary	Guillemont	24/10/1916	27/10/1916
War Diary	Lesboueire	28/10/1916	31/10/1916
War Diary	Briqueterie	01/11/1916	02/11/1916

War Diary	Trones Wood	03/11/1916	05/11/1916
War Diary	Flers Line	06/11/1916	07/11/1916
War Diary	Carnoy	08/11/1916	08/11/1916
War Diary	Meaulte	09/11/1916	11/11/1916
War Diary	Citerne	12/11/1916	08/12/1916
War Diary	Vaux-sur-Somme	08/12/1916	08/12/1916
War Diary	Camp 11	09/12/1916	10/12/1916
War Diary	Camp 17	11/12/1916	13/12/1916
War Diary	Trenches	14/12/1916	21/12/1916
War Diary	Camp 17	22/12/1916	25/12/1916
War Diary	Camp 12	25/12/1916	27/12/1916
War Diary	Epagne	28/12/1916	17/01/1917
War Diary	Camp 112	17/01/1917	18/01/1917
War Diary	Camp 18	19/01/1917	20/01/1917
War Diary	Line	21/01/1917	24/01/1917
War Diary	Howitzer Wood	25/01/1917	26/01/1917
War Diary	Frise Bend	27/01/1917	27/01/1917
War Diary	Line	28/01/1917	30/01/1917
War Diary	Suzanne	31/01/1917	31/01/1917
Miscellaneous	Head General Head Division Bart	01/03/1919	01/03/1919
War Diary	Suzanne	01/02/1917	07/02/1917
War Diary	Support Line	08/02/1917	10/02/1917
War Diary	Support Line	11/02/1917	11/02/1917
War Diary	Line	12/02/1917	16/02/1917
War Diary	Howitzer Wood	15/02/1917	19/02/1917
War Diary	Trenches	20/02/1917	23/02/1917
War Diary	Road Wood	24/02/1917	28/02/1917
War Diary	Camp 19	01/03/1917	08/03/1917
War Diary	Camp 13	09/03/1917	31/03/1917
Miscellaneous	D.A.G. General Headquarters. 3rd Echelon Base.	02/03/1917	02/03/1917
War Diary	Camp 13	01/04/1917	01/04/1917
War Diary	Corbie	02/04/1917	02/04/1917
War Diary	Bertangles	03/04/1917	03/04/1917
War Diary	Beagval	04/04/1917	04/04/1917
War Diary	Lucheux	05/04/1917	06/04/1917
War Diary	Humber Court	07/04/1917	07/04/1917
War Diary	Baillegival	08/04/1917	10/04/1917
War Diary	Mercatel	11/04/1917	11/04/1917
War Diary	Henin	12/04/1917	14/04/1917
War Diary	Hindenbure Line	14/04/1917	27/04/1917
War Diary	Bailleuival	28/04/1917	01/05/1917
War Diary	Monchy Au Bois	03/05/1917	12/05/1917
War Diary	Boisleux St Marc	13/05/1917	15/05/1917
War Diary	Front Line	16/05/1917	21/05/1917
War Diary	St. Leger	22/05/1917	26/05/1917
War Diary	Front Line	27/05/1917	28/05/1917
War Diary	Moyenville	29/05/1917	30/05/1917
War Diary	Bailleulval	31/05/1917	31/05/1917
Miscellaneous	D.A.G. General Headquarters, 3rd Echelon. Base.	01/07/1917	01/07/1917
War Diary	Bailleulval	01/06/1917	17/06/1917
War Diary	Moyenville	18/06/1917	19/06/1917
War Diary	Croisilles	20/06/1917	24/06/1917
War Diary	Moyenville	25/06/1917	29/06/1917
War Diary	Monchy	30/06/1917	30/06/1917
Miscellaneous	D.A.G. General Headquarters. 3rd Echelon Base.	31/07/1917	31/07/1917
War Diary	Monchy Au Bois	01/07/1917	01/07/1917

War Diary	Llealvillers	02/07/1917	02/07/1917
War Diary	Naours	03/07/1917	03/07/1917
War Diary	Bouchon	04/07/1917	04/07/1917
War Diary	Conde	05/07/1917	31/07/1917
War Diary	Bray Dunes	01/08/1917	14/08/1917
War Diary	Coxyde	15/08/1917	15/08/1917
War Diary	Trenches	16/08/1917	27/08/1917
War Diary	La Panne	28/08/1917	29/08/1917
War Diary	Capelle	30/08/1917	31/08/1917
War Diary	Moulle	01/09/1917	28/09/1917
War Diary	Reclinghem	29/09/1917	30/09/1917
War Diary	Racquinghem	01/10/1917	06/10/1917
War Diary	Monninghem	06/10/1917	08/10/1917
War Diary	Line	09/10/1917	12/10/1917
War Diary	Bristol Castle	13/10/1917	14/10/1917
War Diary	Aldershot Camp	15/10/1917	16/10/1917
War Diary	Ypres	17/10/1917	24/10/1917
War Diary	Neuve Eglise	26/10/1917	31/10/1917
War Diary	Line	01/11/1917	04/11/1917
War Diary	Bristol Castle	05/11/1917	07/11/1917
War Diary	Canteen Corner Camp	08/11/1917	16/11/1917
War Diary	Meninroad	16/10/1917	18/10/1917
War Diary	Potijze	19/10/1917	27/10/1917
War Diary	Hamburt	28/10/1917	30/11/1917
War Diary	Brandhoek	01/12/1917	04/12/1917
War Diary	St Jean	05/12/1917	11/12/1917
War Diary	Wattou	11/12/1917	22/12/1917
War Diary	Hlvation Corner	22/12/1917	27/12/1917
War Diary	Watou Area	28/12/1917	31/12/1917
War Diary	Watou	01/01/1918	06/01/1918
War Diary	Line	07/01/1918	08/01/1918
War Diary	Brandhoek	09/01/1918	12/01/1918
War Diary	Support Line Seinf	12/01/1918	12/01/1918
War Diary	Seine	14/01/1918	17/01/1918
War Diary	Line	17/01/1918	19/01/1918
War Diary	Toronto Camp	20/01/1918	20/01/1918
War Diary	Brandhoek	21/01/1918	21/01/1918
War Diary	Toronto Camp	22/01/1918	26/01/1918
War Diary	Brandhoek	27/01/1918	31/01/1918
War Diary	St Martin Au Leart	01/02/1918	20/02/1918
War Diary	Ypres	21/02/1918	21/02/1918
War Diary	Passchendaele	21/02/1918	24/02/1918
War Diary	Whithy Camp	25/02/1918	28/02/1918
War Diary	Passchendaele	01/03/1918	05/03/1918
War Diary	Whitby Camp	05/03/1918	08/03/1918
War Diary	Line	09/03/1918	15/03/1918
War Diary	Aiden Camp	16/03/1918	20/03/1918
War Diary	Brandhoek	20/03/1918	20/03/1918
War Diary	Line	21/03/1918	27/03/1918
War Diary	Beandhoek	28/03/1918	31/03/1918
Heading	19th Brigade. 33rd Division. 1st Battalion Cameronians (Scottish Rifles) April 1918		
War Diary	Grand Rullecourt	01/04/1918	05/04/1918
War Diary	Y Camp	06/04/1918	07/04/1918
War Diary	Grande Rullecourt	08/04/1918	11/04/1918
War Diary	Meteren	12/04/1918	30/04/1918

War Diary	St Marie Cappelle	01/05/1918	01/05/1918
War Diary	Racqingham	02/05/1918	03/05/1918
War Diary	Camp Near Abeelie	04/05/1918	05/05/1918
War Diary	Atlantle Camp.	06/05/1918	11/05/1918
War Diary	Diary Buenet Corner	12/05/1918	12/05/1918
War Diary	Dirty Bucket	13/05/1918	18/05/1918
War Diary	Camp at L 8 d 92. Sheet 27	19/05/1918	20/05/1918
War Diary	Bois De St Acaire	21/05/1918	24/05/1918
War Diary	Poperinghe	25/05/1918	03/06/1918
War Diary	6.7. a. 9.6.	04/06/1918	07/06/1918
War Diary	Belgian Battery Corner	08/06/1918	10/06/1918
War Diary	Line	11/06/1918	15/06/1918
War Diary	Erie Camp	16/06/1918	20/06/1918
War Diary	Line	21/06/1918	30/06/1918
War Diary	Brandhoek	01/07/1918	05/07/1918
War Diary	Canal	06/07/1918	15/07/1918
War Diary	Brandhoek	16/07/1918	20/07/1918
War Diary	Canal	21/07/1918	31/07/1918
War Diary	Vlamertinghe Green Line	01/08/1918	15/08/1918
War Diary	Crainsford	16/08/1918	19/08/1918
War Diary	Lieques	20/08/1918	26/08/1918
War Diary	Appendix A		
War Diary		26/08/1918	28/08/1918
War Diary	Ivergny	29/08/1918	14/09/1918
War Diary	Etricourt	15/09/1918	15/09/1918
War Diary	V. 218.22	16/09/1918	18/09/1918
War Diary	W20	19/09/1918	21/09/1918
War Diary		22/09/1918	26/09/1918
War Diary	V-17 X 13	27/09/1918	30/09/1918
War Diary	Vauclette Farm	01/10/1918	02/10/1918
War Diary	Canal De L'escaut	03/10/1918	05/10/1918
War Diary	Ossus	05/10/1918	05/10/1918
War Diary	Kinbston Quarry	05/10/1918	05/10/1918
War Diary	Hindenbure Line	05/10/1918	07/10/1918
War Diary	Le Catellat Nauroyline	08/10/1918	09/10/1918
War Diary	Deheries	09/10/1918	09/10/1918
War Diary	Bertry	09/10/1918	09/10/1918
War Diary	Troisville	09/10/1918	11/10/1918
War Diary	Malincourt	12/10/1918	18/10/1918
War Diary	Troisvilles	19/10/1918	22/10/1918
War Diary	K10 B 11c	23/10/1918	23/10/1918
War Diary	K 15 C & d	24/10/1918	24/10/1918
War Diary	Les Tvilleries	25/10/1918	25/10/1918
War Diary	Troisvillers	26/10/1918	03/11/1918
War Diary	Eagelontain	04/11/1918	04/11/1918
War Diary	Foxetde Mormal	05/11/1918	06/11/1918
War Diary	Petit Maubeuge	06/11/1918	06/11/1918
War Diary	Pot de Vin	07/11/1918	07/11/1918
War Diary	Sabaras	08/11/1918	11/11/1918
War Diary	Berlaimont	12/11/1918	14/11/1918
War Diary	Locquignol	15/11/1918	15/11/1918
War Diary	Croix	16/11/1918	16/11/1918
War Diary	Clary	17/11/1918	09/12/1918
War Diary	Masixieres	11/12/1918	11/12/1918
War Diary	Hermies	12/12/1918	12/12/1918
War Diary	Faureuil	13/12/1918	13/12/1918

War Diary	Alrert	14/12/1918	14/12/1918
War Diary	Pont Noyelles	15/12/1918	15/12/1918
War Diary	Ailly	16/12/1918	16/12/1918
War Diary	Lincheux	17/12/1918	13/01/1919
War Diary	Rouen	14/01/1919	24/05/1919

WO 95 2422/2

1 Bn Cameronians (R. Scottish Rifles)

Dec 1915 – May 1919

33RD DIVISION
19TH INFY BDE

1ST BN SCOTTISH RIFLES
(CAMERONIANS)
DEC 1916 - MAY 1919

FROM 2 DIV 19 BDE

33RD DIVISION
19TH INFY BDE

√XXXIII 18th Roy / Scottish Rifles
Dec
Vol XVII

WAR DIARY
or
INTELLIGENCE SUMMARY.

Army Form C. 2118.

1/1 Bn 77e Canadians

Place	Date	Hour	Summary of Events and Information	Remarks and references to Appendices
Trenches Canal Sect. "H" (Canal)	1915 Dec 1		handed over trenches relieving Batt". Yorkshire Reg", 7th Div. The 5th Bn. went in on our right & the 18/Royal Fusiliers on our left. Trenches in most awful state. Everything had been allowed to go. No cover or shelter for half the men. No stores handed over properly. about 6f.w. enemy had a gas alarm, horns & whistles were blown & rifle fire was light.	
"	2.		Enemy quiet except a little shelling. All companies busy getting his chis opened up. Major Selby Lownde attached & a Lt. from 15 Hussars.	
"	3		Enemy quiet. Own gun asking Huns upper hand in craters. 3 men slightly wounded (2 or duty) by his own Trench mortar.	
"	4		Enemy shells support his chis. busy wet and Trenches falling in everywhere. All companies non & a lot of work. A few men been told with their feet which

WAR DIARY
or
INTELLIGENCE SUMMARY.
(Erase heading not required.)

Army Form C. 2118.

Place	Date	Hour	Summary of Events and Information	Remarks and references to Appendices
Trenches Curlu Salient N of Armentières	1915 Dec.		is accounted for by there being no Seig. only, & therefore it is practically impossible to obtain & get them from back trenches etc. The Trenches are kept as tidy as last year which need not have been the case. Pte Bell killed & Tonkin wounded.	
	5.		Enemy much more active. All support trenches shelled & windy corner. One man killed Pte Clark & Pte Martin wounded. Very wet & trenches falling in as quickly as built up. A lot of work done. The 2/5 know is road getting in & is passable.	
Billets Aurichy	6		Relieved by R. Welsh Fus at 10.30 a.m. & Batt. went into very dirty Billets in Aurichy. Durnis & Perrow on him there the 3rd & 5th R.R's were in arm 2nd Plat & the 18th Royal Fus were on our left. The latter are Kitchener army & have not yet learnt to turn their backs adverse by night	

Army Form C. 2118.

WAR DIARY
or
INTELLIGENCE SUMMARY.
(Erase heading not required.)

Place	Date	Hour	Summary of Events and Information	Remarks and references to Appendices
Billets Quesnoy	1915 Dec 7		6 Platoons in R.E. fatigue by night & one by day. Being cleaning of billets taken over from Indians left in the most filthy condition imaginable. A lot of spare boots found lying about.	
Billets le Quesnoy	Dec 8		The same large fatigue parties were found by day and night. The weather was so bad that the men had very little chance to get clean or even dry, work continued on the billets, drawing and constructing permanent latrines & washhouses.	
Billets le Quesnoy	Dec 9		Major Stormonth-Darling who had been Adjutant of the battalion since Mobilization 1913 left us to take command of the 9th A.S.L. Work continued on the billets but no parties had to be found for R.E. fatigue.	
Billets HAMEN ARTOIS	Dec 10		The battalion marched back to Flers en-Artois a small village about 3 kilometres from LILLERS. The distance was about 13 miles and in spite of having had	

Army Form C. 2118.

WAR DIARY
or
INTELLIGENCE SUMMARY.

(Erase heading not required.)

Instructions regarding War Diaries and Intelligence Summaries are contained in F. S. Regs., Part II. and the Staff Manual respectively. Title pages will be prepared in manuscript.

Place	Date	Hour	Summary of Events and Information	Remarks and references to Appendices
Hameau des Billets	Dec 11		Hardly any rest since the 1st. The men marched very well. Billets rather scattered.	
Billets Hameau de Billets	Dec 12		Day spent in cleaning clothes and equipment. Rain very heavy and some of the billets flooded. 2/Lt Brownlie joined the Battalion.	
Tillé Hameautin	Dec 13		2/Lt Rhodes? joined the Battalion. Some of the billets had to be evacuated owing to floods. But others were easily found. Work was begun on the billets under direction of Pioneer Sergeant. Beds were put up in the barns and permanent washhouses and latrines constructed.	
Billets Hameau des Billets	Dec 14		2/Lt Powell joined the battalion. Weather cold and dry. Training carried on as usual, though drill fields very small and bad.	

Army Form C. 2118.

WAR DIARY
or
INTELLIGENCE SUMMARY.
(Erase heading not required.)

Place	Date	Hour	Summary of Events and Information	Remarks and references to Appendices
Billets Hamel-les-Lillers	Dec 15		Captain Hill left the Battalion for the 33rd Divisional School of Instruction as a temporary instructor. Company training carried out and training of specialist squads in the use of Lewis machine gun commenced.	
Billets Hamel-les-Lillers	Dec 16		Battalion Foot-ball in a short Brigade route march marched past the Divisional General.	
Billets Hamel-les-Lillers	Dec 17		Programme of training carried out as usual.	
Billets HAMEL-en-ARTOIS	Dec 18		The wet weather and state of the ground made training very difficult.	
Billets Hamel-en-Artois	Dec 19		Church Parade services for Church of England and Church of Scotland were held in billets, and Roman Catholic mass at H.A.M. Church.	

Army Form C. 2118.

WAR DIARY
or
INTELLIGENCE SUMMARY.
(Erase heading not required.)

Place	Date	Hour	Summary of Events and Information	Remarks and references to Appendices
Billets Hamenlis Dec	20th Dec		Training by companies carried out and work on billets continued. Much more work could have been done if more material had been available.	
Billets Hamenlis Dec	21st Dec		Weather very wet and most of the fields swamped making training a matter of some difficulty.	
Billets Hamenlis Dec	22nd Dec		The battalion received four machine guns towards the full establishment of two per platoon.	
Billets Hamen Artois Dec	23rd Dec		Platoons were inspected in full marching order by company commanders.	
Billets Hamen Artois Dec	24th Dec		A battalion route march was arranged, but had to be cancelled owing to rain.	

Army Form C. 2118.

WAR DIARY
or
INTELLIGENCE SUMMARY.

(Erase heading not required.)

Instructions regarding War Diaries and Intelligence Summaries are contained in F. S. Regs., Part II. and the Staff Manual respectively. Title pages will be prepared in manuscript.

Place	Date	Hour	Summary of Events and Information	Remarks and references to Appendices
Billes Hanuches Dec	25th		A Christmas dinner was given to the battalion consisting of roast pork, vegetables and beer, supplemented by plum-pudding and other gifts from home.	
Billes Hamachatle Dec	26th		Church services were held for Church of England and Roman Catholics and baths were obtained for the whole battalion. Two companies going to BOSHES and two to BOUREEQ.	
Billes Hamachatle Dec ANNEZIN	27th		The battalion moved to ANNEZIN near BETHUNE on the way back to the trenches, a march of about 10 miles but transport was secured for the men's packs.	
Billes ANNEQUIN	28th Dec		4th battalion moved up Close reserve billets in ANNEQUIN South of the LA BASSÉE road.	

WAR DIARY
or
INTELLIGENCE SUMMARY.
(Erase heading not required.)

Army Form C. 2118.

Place	Date	Hour	Summary of Events and Information	Remarks and references to Appendices
Trenches	29th Dec		Major T.O.C. Hamilton left the Bn. to take command of the 2/4 Royal Fusiliers. The battalion relieved the 5th Kings Liverpools in subsection 2.0 just north of HOHENZOLLERN REDOUBT. Three companies B,C,A. from left to right were in the first line. B Coy had one platoon in B'91 reserve line and one platoon in RAILWAY KEEP. The trenches were in bad repair, we had been for some months, but a lot of work was required the 19th. Under which we were in our right and the shelling was R.W. Fletcher in dept. 2 Lt. J.J. Reynolds severely wounded by a shell in one of the communication trenches were only "quiet" here except for shelling with field guns.	
Trenches	30th Dec.			
Trenches	31st Dec.		2 Lt J.J. Reynolds died of wounds in BETHUNE. We had but considerable amount of shelling each night. Although enemy's Machine gun was active. No 9168 a REMT and No. 6558 R.Q.S KENNEDY killed by a shell in a road in rear of the trenches.	signed [illegible] Lt Col Commanding the [illegible]

Army Form C. 2118.

WAR DIARY of 1st Battalion
The Cameronians
INTELLIGENCE SUMMARY.
(Erase heading not required.)

Places	Date	Hour	Summary of Events and Information	Remarks and references to Appendices
Trenches	1st Jan. 1916		The work in progress chiefly consisted of clearing communication trenches which had apparently been left untouched since 25th September. R.E. material was very hard to obtain. No: 7164 Pte WEILSON wounded and No: SPEIGHT wounded.	15 M. 11 sheets
Trenches	2nd Jan.		Enemy fairly quiet. Our snipers did a considerable amount of work wounding a German and hitting a periscope.	
Trenches	3rd Jany.		We fired rifle grenades at intervals during the night to which the enemy made a feeble reply. Sgt No: 6216 Sgt: Irvine wounded	
Trenches	4th Jany		Battalion relieved by 5th Scottish Rifles. Rifleman FOSSE. A. (private) died of wounds was also in the Trenches but no footbridge and very little barbed	

WAR DIARY
or
INTELLIGENCE SUMMARY.

Place	Date	Hour	Summary of Events and Information	Remarks and references to Appendices
Rue des ANNEQUIN	5th Jany		could be obtained. The battalion received 10,750 Sandbags, 22 shields of corrugated iron, 170 pickets, 20 chevaux de frise, 10 coils of barbed wire, 30 lengths of sheeting, 250 feet of planking. For more than this could have been disposed of. This was the first time we had Lewis guns in the trenches and they seemed to give the men a great deal of confidence. The weather was good.	
"	6th		6 Platoons working on communication trenches - enemy shelled billets slightly with field guns	
			8 Platoons working on communication trenches.	
"	7th		The same working parties were found. C Company were supplying Picquet.	

Place	Date	Hour	Summary of Events and Information	Remarks and references to Appendices
Bethune	8th		The Bn. moved into Billets in the Rue D'Aire. The billets were the same that the Bn. was in before. They have been much improved by the erection by R.E. of proper latrines and washing places — the floors being cemented and the water chained off. The only wonder is that this had not been done before.	
	9th		Sunday — Divine service held.	
	10th		Companies carried out fires under Company arrangements. Running Drill, Smoke Helmet Drill, & Fire Control, Bomb & Lewis Gun training was also carried out. Captain Hill rejoined the Bn. from Hospital on this date. There was an afternoon parade for young Officers & N.C.Os at 2 p.m.	

Army Form C. 2118.

WAR DIARY
or
INTELLIGENCE SUMMARY.
(Erase heading not required.)

Place	Date	Hour	Summary of Events and Information	Remarks and references to Appendices
	11th		Still under Company arrangements. Every man has now been issued with two Tube Helmets and a pair of goggles.	
	12th		The Commanding Officer attended a Lecture at AIRE. Still under Company arrangements. The weather has been fine for the last few days but cold.	
	13th		Baths at the ECOLE DE JEUNE FILLES were detailed to Coys. The Commanding Officer & Company Commanders went round the trenches in A.2. The B.G. relieves the 2/ Worcester Regt. tomorrow.	Recce Extract Quartering Arrangements

2353 Wt. W 2544/1454 700,000 5/15 D. D. & L. A.D.S.S./Forms/C. 2118.

Army Form C. 2118.

WAR DIARY
or
INTELLIGENCE SUMMARY.
(Erase heading not required.)

Instructions regarding War Diaries and Intelligence Summaries are contained in F. S. Regs., Part II. and the Staff Manual respectively. Title pages will be prepared in manuscript.

Place	Date	Hour	Summary of Events and Information	Remarks and references to Appendices
Trenches Montauban (Carnoy)				
Guinchy (A.2.)	14th		The Bn. relieved the 2/Worcesters at 5.30 p.m. in the A.2. sector. The 18th Royal Fusiliers are in A.1. and the 20th Royal Fusiliers in B.1. in rear of the Canal. Two Companies (A & D) were in the firing line, one Cy. (C.) in Support and one Cy. (B) in Reserve at PONT FIXE. N⁰ 6500 L/Cpl. Buckley was killed.	
	15.		Inspection of the Trenches today. Thus them to be in a fearful condition. The crater portion of the line has been abandoned altogether. There is no communication between A & B Coys, and the trenches have been allowed to fall in and dangerous and no effort being made to redeem them. Enemy as using large minenwerfer against B. Coy. N⁰ 16148 Pte Tattersall wounded.	

WAR DIARY
or
INTELLIGENCE SUMMARY.
(Erase heading not required.)

Army Form C. 2118.

Place	Date	Hour	Summary of Events and Information	Remarks and references to Appendices
	16.		The enemy artillery has been very active lately. There has been a fairly continous shelling of the front line, supports, and PONT FIXE with 5.9" and field guns. "B" Coy were severely shelled with minenwerfer - one of which buried seven men - none of them being hurt. A Rifle Grenade falling in "A" Coy trench killed No. 8946. L/Cpl. Dawe and No. 8831 Pte Mahon and wounded No. 16763 Pte Cummings 16720 Pte Howarth and 9426 Pte Williams. The heavy artillery replied in retaliation to the minenwerfer. In spite of the continued shelling by the enemy a large amount of work was done by Companies. Three platoons of "D" Coy were moved up to the Central leaving one platoon at PONT FIXE. No 16177 Sgt Burch was wounded also 11177 Pte Cunningham. Headquarters received a few shells, the Hollow & the Bulge were also shelled with field guns and 5.9" Hows:	
	17.			

Army Form C. 2118.

WAR DIARY
or
INTELLIGENCE SUMMARY.
(Erase heading not required.)

Instructions regarding War Diaries and Intelligence Summaries are contained in F.S. Regs., Part II. and the Staff Manual respectively. Title pages will be prepared in manuscript.

Place	Date	Hour	Summary of Events and Information	Remarks and references to Appendices
	18th		Continual work was carried on night & day with the ulmer object. The trenches are once more assuming their proper form. Communication was established along the whole front line. This was later locked by their evening 5.9" shells that fell in the front line completely filling the trench. B Coy also suffered from the effects of Minnenwerfer fire. — JERUSALEM HILL being blown in. Gun artillery both heavy & light retaliated vigorously. No. 8721 Pte King was wounded.	
	19th		Continual shelling by both sides. The trenches are a lot better, but there is a colossal amount of work yet to be done. The BULGE was blown in — the Lewis machine gunners had a remarkable escape. The Bridge was completed between "A" Coy & the Centre Coy Cemy. No casualties.	

WAR DIARY
or
INTELLIGENCE SUMMARY.

Army Form C. 2118.

Place	Date	Hour	Summary of Events and Information	Remarks and references to Appendices
	26th		No. 9333 Sgr Mercer was killed and 7513 Pte McFarlane wounded. We were relieved by the 2/Royal Irish Fusiliers at 5:30 p.m. The following is the amount of R.E. material used by the Bn. during this period in the trenches. We go to ANNEQUIN. NORTH.	
			Sandbags .... 21,000.	
			Quartering ...... 575 feet	
			Wooden Hurdles 120.	
			Nails .... 29 lbs	
			Barbed wire ..... 25 coils	
			Plain wire .... 5 coils	
			Fascines 185	
			Pickets .... 110.	
			Planking .... 400 feet	
			Chevaux de Frise 18.	
			CAPT. DREW rejoined the Bn. on this date.	

Lieut. Col.
Commanding 1/Cameronians

Army Form C. 2118.

WAR DIARY
or
INTELLIGENCE SUMMARY.
(Erase heading not required.)

Instructions regarding War Diaries and Intelligence Summaries are contained in F. S. Regs., Part II. and the Staff Manual respectively. Title pages will be prepared in manuscript.

Place	Date	Hour	Summary of Events and Information	Remarks and references to Appendices
ANNEQUIN (NORTH).	21st		We occupied the billets that we held before, when in this place. The billets are not good, and are scattered – they were however clean. We have all the Bn except 1 Coy on fatigues. The one Coy is ready to move at five minutes notice – the Bn at half + hour – but with the remaining Coys on fatigues in the trenches this seems very unlikely. The Commanding Officer went on leave this morning.	
	22nd		The B'n with the exception of the Bulging Company were on fatigues.	
	23rd		"D" Coy went into the trenches in A1. in order to bring the 20th Royal Fusiliers up to strength – they having 200 men + officers at CHOQUES guarding the Divisional Staff. A voluntary Church of England Service was held. The whole Bn got baths and a clean change of underclothing today.	

WAR DIARY or INTELLIGENCE SUMMARY.

Army Form C. 2118.

Place	Date	Hour	Summary of Events and Information	Remarks and references to Appendices
	24.		The Bttn. with the exception of the Helping Company were on fatigues	
	25.		" " "	
	26.		" " "	
	27.		Today was the Kaisers Birthday, we therefore expected an attack or some shelling. However everything passed quietly. The 80 rule the trenches tomorrow for three days.	
	28.		We relieved the Royal Welsh Fusiliers at 5.30 p.m. They had been trouble with MINENWERFER and had a fair amount of casualties. Otherwise things were quiet.	(A2)
	29.		At 9.45 am the Germans exploded a mine on the South side of the LA BASSÉE ROAD in Z. Section. This started the Artillery on both sides firing and for five hours the sections A1. & A2 were shelled heavily by the enemy.	

WAR DIARY
or
INTELLIGENCE SUMMARY.

(Erase heading not required.)

Army Form C. 2118.

Place	Date	Hour	Summary of Events and Information	Remarks and references to Appendices
	29th (cont)		It was one of the most sustained bombardments since LA BOUTILLERIE. HUNTER ST - OLDRENT ROAD. CABBAGE PATCH & COLDSTREAM LANE were shelled at an period and telephone communication with the left Coy ("B") and the right Coy ("E") was destroyed. The wire to "B" Coy was completely spared and a new wire had to be laid. Our Artillery replied vigorously and in the end silenced the meddling of the enemy.	
	30th		We were relieved by the 1st Middlesex Regiment at 4.30 p.m. We marched from the trenches to MONTMORENCY BARRACKS in BETHUNE.	
	31st		The Bn was in two hours notice. The day was spent in cleaning kit and inspections.	

Lieut Colonel
Comdg 11 Battalion The Cameronians

XXXIII 2/33
   19
1 Scottish Rifles
Vol XVIII
~~XIX~~

Army Form C. 2118.

WAR DIARY 1/1 Battalion
or
INTELLIGENCE SUMMARY. The Cameronian
(Erase heading not required.)

16.M
9 weeks

Place	Date	Hour	Summary of Events and Information	Remarks and references to Appendices
BILLETS BETHUNE	Feb 1st		Companies carried out Physical Training, Route March &c. Instructions were received for the movement of the Battalion by rail to HAM &c on the 4th for Divisional Training.	
	2nd		Companies training. Commanding Officer inspected Regimental transport, whose turn-out was exceptionally good.	
	3rd		Companies route-marched & carried out training in musketry. Orders for movement of Battalion to HAM cancelled.	
	4th		Companies training in musketry & general fighting. Orders received for the battalion to go into the trenches tomorrow in Z 1 section.	
	5th		The Commanding Officer & Company Commanders visited trenches of Z 1 in the morning. Just as the leading parties of the battalion were about to move off the relief was cancelled; the orders for relief are to take effect tomorrow.	

WAR DIARY
or
INTELLIGENCE SUMMARY.

Army Form C. 2118.

Place	Date	Hour	Summary of Events and Information	Remarks and references to Appendices
TRENCHES Z.1 CAMBRIN	July 5th	6ᵃ	Battalion took over Z.1 subsection from the 16th Bn K.R.R. holding the line with two companies (A & B), two companies (C & D) in billets in BEUVRY. The two keeps SIMS KEEP & ARTHURS KEEP were held by one platoon each of the companies in the line in front. The 1st QUEENS were on our right, 2.0 & the 2nd WORCESTERS on our left in Z.2. The night passed quietly in the front line, but Headquarters were shelled throughout the night by field guns = 4.2.s	
	6th		The trenches were damp but a lot of work was needed on the bonjours & many were unsafe. Deep dugouts in HIGH STREET had, for some reason, been allowed to fall into disrepair; these were cleared out & taken into use during the next few days. From about 3 pm to 5 pm the enemy shelled the whole of the subsection, with particular attention to the bonjours, cutting the telephone wires to each of the companies in several places; we had no casualties. Our Artillery retaliated heavily.	
	7th		Work chiefly consisted of repairing the damage of yesterday's bombardment, though all trenches had been made passable the same night. D Company was brought up	

Army Form C. 2118.

WAR DIARY
or
INTELLIGENCE SUMMARY.
(Erase heading not required.)

Place	Date	Hour	Summary of Events and Information	Remarks and references to Appendices
TRENCHES Z.1 CAMBRIN	8th Continued		from BEUVRY to take over the two huts, thus giving one more platoon to each of the companies in the front line. Work was started on deep dugouts in the front line, which previously had nothing which gave any cover. The 2nd R.W.F. to our left, the 5th Scottish Rifles Z.2 on our right.	
	9th		Enemy quiet, allowing us to get on well with work; our guns were very active, & sent over a lot of heavy shells.	
	10th		A company of the 7th (or 74th?) LEINSTER REGIMENT attached to the battalion for instruction & put into the trenches in relief of "B" Company who marched back to BEUVRY billets. Enemy were quiet on our front.	
	11th		A quiet day. The dug-outs in HIGH STREET and mens in use & the trench itself have been built up & put in good repair. The field of fire from ARTHUR'S KEEP is very limited & a good deal of levelling is necessary; this work was started on at dark. No.10965 Sergt W. LINNEY was killed while the Sapping Platoon was working at this.	

WAR DIARY
or
INTELLIGENCE SUMMARY.
(Erase heading not required.)

Army Form C. 2118.

Place	Date	Hour	Summary of Events and Information	Remarks and references to Appendices
TRENCHES Z1 CAMBRIN	Sat 12th Feb		The enemy shelled us heavily with field guns & 5.9's from about 2pm to 5pm doing considerable damage to the parapet & support line, cutting the wires from both companies in the front line & from the h.q's. 2nd Lt. 5717 Regt Sgt Major T. WINDERAM was wounded. Two men killed, 7406 Pte W. Campbell & 11039 Pte W. Pitts, & five wounded 18820 Pte J. Thomson, 11281 Pte J. Burns, 8567 Cpl B. Good, 9067 Pte R. Coughlin. All communication trenches had been made passable shortly after dark. A "B" Coy relieved the company of the LEINSTERS. 2nd Lieut Rogers joined the battalion.	
	Sun 13th		The enemy again bombarded us with field guns & 5.9's from 1pm to 4pm, doing most damage to the communication trenches round ARTHUR'S KEEP. Our guns retaliated heavily & still bombarded the enemy after he had ceased firing. R. 10849 Pte R. ORAM was wounded.	
	Mon 14th		A great deal of work was put in repairing the damage done by the bombardments of the two previous days & some rain during the night. The day passed quietly except for half an hour in the morning when work round ARTHUR'S KEEP was	

Army Form C. 2118.

WAR DIARY
or
INTELLIGENCE SUMMARY.
(Erase heading not required.)

Place	Date	Hour	Summary of Events and Information	Remarks and references to Appendices
TRENCHES CAMBRIN Z.1.	Feb 14th Continued		Steadily a sharp bombardment with shrapnel. "B" Company relieved "D" Company in the trenches.	
	Tues 15th		Last night there was two hours snow followed by rain which caused a good many falls in the communication trenches & the whole day was taken up in working on the falls. The deep dug-outs in the front line are progressing slowly, it is very difficult to get the necessary material from the R.E.'s who are unfortunately making similar dugouts close by for machine gunners & need most of the available material for their own work.	
	Wed 16th		The day passed quietly & a lot of work was got through. The front line is now in very good condition throughout its length, the parapet, fire step, & traverses have been revetted in many places with sandbags & the floor of the trench is built up afresh, "D" Company relieved "C" Company who marched back to billets in BEUVRY. The moonlight was very bright almost the whole night, which interfered with the patrolling & our wiring parties.	

WAR DIARY
or
INTELLIGENCE SUMMARY.

(Erase heading not required.)

Army Form C. 2118.

Place	Date	Hour	Summary of Events and Information	Remarks and references to Appendices
TRENCHES CAMBRIN 2.1.	Thurs Aug 17th		A quiet day for us, I not for the enemy. Our trenches are in good condition now, with the exception of MAISON ROUGE ALLEY, so that we ought to be able to hand them over to-morrow in good order. Our heavy artillery bombarded AUCHY & the DUMP most of the afternoon, the enemy did not retaliate.	
	Fri 18th		Battalion relieved by the 2nd R.W.F., after twelve days in this subsection. Battalion moved back to billets at ANNEQUIN (SOUTH).	
BILLETS ANNEQUIN (SOUTH)	Sat 19th		Billets in pretty dirty condition. Turned all hands in getting this put right. No what men were left after supplying the numerous working parties called for.	
	Sun 20th		Greater part of battalion on working parties in the trenches; companies had the use of the baths in ANNEQUIN NORTH	
	Mon 21st		A party of about 80 men were left behind to carry on working parties till midnight — the remainder of the battalion moved off in the afternoon to billets near OBLINGHEM	

Army Form C. 2118.

WAR DIARY
or
INTELLIGENCE SUMMARY.

(Erase heading not required.)

Place	Date	Hour	Summary of Events and Information	Remarks and references to Appendices
BILLETS				
OBLINGHEM	Mon 21st	Continued	The last company reached billets about 9 p.m.	
	Tues 22nd		This place has only very recently been taken over as a billeting area & has no little stone or permanent sanitary arrangements. Our pioneers are starting to remedy the same & we propose to put up permanent latrines, cook houses, & erect as many wire beds in the billets as time permits.	
	Wed 23rd		Sharp frost last night followed by snow in the early morning which continued all day falling as sleet. No out-of-door training for the companies except for route marching.	
	Thurs 24th		Snow continued with frost a 15° of F, making the roads very slippery. Companies carried out musketry instruction & physical training under difficult conditions.	
	Fri 25th		Snow & frost. Commanding Officer inspected the Regimental Transport.	
	Sat 26th		Same weather conditions prevailed. Companies doing their best to carry out training.	

WAR DIARY
or
INTELLIGENCE SUMMARY.
(Erase heading not required.)

Army Form C. 2118.

Place	Date	Hour	Summary of Events and Information	Remarks and references to Appendices
BILLETS OBLINGHEM	Sun 27th		Divine Service for all denominations was held in the largest billet, at various hours during the day.	
	Mon 28th		Snow & slush. Companies training under difficulties.	
	Tues 29th		" " " " "	
	March 1st		" " " " "	
ANNEQUIN NORTH			Battalion moved up to billets in ANNEQUIN NORTH preparatory to going into trenches to-morrow.	
	Thurs 2nd		Battalion moved up to trenches relieving 6th Bn. Scottish Rifles in the CUINCHY Section A.2 sub sector of the CANAL. The trenches were in a pretty bad state from the recent terrible weather and as the 6th Sco. Rif. were very weak they had had more than they could compete with. No. 11084 Pte. J. THOMPSON wounded.	

WAR DIARY of 1st Battn. The Cameronians (Scottish Rifles)

INTELLIGENCE SUMMARY

Place	Date	Hour	Summary of Events and Information	Remarks and references to Appendices
TRENCHES CUINCHY A2	March 2nd 3rd		The Companies are posted "D" Coy front Right, "B" Coy front Left, "C" Coy front Reserve, "A" Coy in reserve. Companies worked hard last night & to-day at the whole system of trenches & is beginning to look in very fair condition; if the weather holds we shall soon have them good. On the whole the enemy has been quiet; about mid-day a few trench mortars were sent over into the brickstacks but no damage was done. The bombers & sapping platoon are going to start to-night on the saps, as the rumours are very anxious to have them pushed out far enough to prevent enemy patrols leaving our sapping morning work.	
	3rd		St Chaffin's day. By mid-day all the trenches were clear & clean, but in the early afternoon thick snow started again & rapidly changed things. By night the mud was thick again in spite of all efforts. The sapping work was almost helpless owing to the wet & the crumbling nature of the earth. From the many rumours being in the vicinity. The enemy sent over a few trench mortar bombs in reply to our own, among the BRICKSTACKS. 8170 Pte H. OWENS & 7537 Pte D. MACKIE were wounded. We have got the 33rd Divisional Artillery behind us now & they are very	

WAR DIARY
or
INTELLIGENCE SUMMARY.

Army Form C. 2118.

1st S Rifles

Place	Date	Hour	Summary of Events and Information	Remarks and references to Appendices
TRENCHES CUINCHY A2	Sat 4th March Continued		anxious to do their bit for us.	
	Sun 5th		The bad weather continued. The trenches are in a terrible state in spite of all work. Parts of COLDSTREAM LANE & COCKSHY LANE are practically impassable, but we have managed to keep OLD KENT ROAD open, & a way to the front line via PUDDING LANE & the CABBAGE PATCH. The left company have been fortunate & their way is clear all the way up. The sapping work is at a standstill owing to the state of the ground & the bombers are hoping in vain that has already been done, while the sapping platoon has been more usefully employed in working on communication trenches. The whole front line is beginning to settle in, nothing short of solid timber will hold up ground of this sort under bad weather conditions. The enemy sent over some trench mortars after shells near JERUSALEM HILL, one of them killing 7271 Pte P. CAIRNIE & damaging a Lewis gun, 9644 Sgt. A MARTIN was wounded & 2/Lieut A.H MACDONALD, the officer in charge of observation post was killed by a sniper.	

Army Form C. 2118.

1st S Rifles

WAR DIARY
or
INTELLIGENCE SUMMARY.
(Erase heading not required.)

Instructions regarding War Diaries and Intelligence Summaries are contained in F. S. Regs., Part II. and the Staff Manual respectively. Title pages will be prepared in manuscript.

Place	Date	Hour	Summary of Events and Information	Remarks and references to Appendices
TRENCHES CUINCHY A2	Mar 6		Weather still bad. The battalion was relieved at dusk by the 2nd R.W.F. & was marched back to billets in ANNEQUIN (NORTH). The following amount of R.E. material was used by the battalion during this tour of duty in the trenches.	
			Sandbags 9000	
			Barbed wire (coils) 18	
			Footboards 125	
			Hurdles 45	
			Pickets 12	
			Saps (No) 4	
			Loophole plates 16	
			Chevaux de frise 12	
			Planking 470 ft	
			Quartering 160 ft	
			Corrugated iron 2 sheets	

Army Form C. 2118.

WAR DIARY
or
INTELLIGENCE SUMMARY.
(Erase heading not required.)

1st J Rifles

Place	Date	Hour	Summary of Events and Information	Remarks and references to Appendices
BILLETS ANNEQUIN (NORTH)	March Tues 7		Billets in good condition. Those men not taken for working parties went to the baths in ANNEQUIN NORTH.	
	Wed 8		Nearly the whole battalion on working parties under R.E. etc in the trenches. Remainder employed in constructing & improving existing shelters in case of shelling.	
	Thurs 9			
	Fri 10			
	Sat 11		At dusk the battalion relieved the 2nd R.W.F. in trenches in the CUINCHY (A2) subsection. The 5th B. Scottish Rifles were on our right & the 20th Royal Fusiliers on our left, north of the canal. The Companies were disposed as follows:— Right Coy. "A" Coy. Centre Coy. "C" Coy. Left Coy. "B" Coy. Reserve Coy "D" Coy. The 2nd R.W.F. had done a lot of work on the trenches. The night passed quietly.	

Army Form C. 2118.

WAR DIARY
or
INTELLIGENCE SUMMARY.
(Erase heading not required.)

1st S Rifles

Place	Date	Hour	Summary of Events and Information	Remarks and references to Appendices
TRENCHES COUCHY LEFT SUBSECTION	March Sun 12th		A quiet day. The enemy sent over six trench mortar bombs into the BRICKSTACKS which did no damage. One of our Lewis guns on the left of the railway embankment killed a German last night & another this morning. The work of the sapping platoon & the bombers is going on in the safe in a more satisfactory way, as the weather is better than we were in trenches last time.	
	Mon 13th		The enemy sent over some minenwerfer bombs & rifle grenades about 2pm but no damage was done. We have now taken over more of the line to our right up to Bayou 32 exclusive from the 5. Scottish Rifles: this includes a saft. The new part of the line is in bad condition, but the rest of the system of trenches is rapidly becoming good, as the last days & nights have been fine. We are digging up a new trench on the south side of the embankment which has a field of fire right up the RAILWAY HOLLOW. Our artillery have started to cut the gaps in the enemy's wire, the gaps are to be kept open at night by our Lewis guns.	

Army Form C. 2118.

WAR DIARY
or
INTELLIGENCE SUMMARY.

(Erase heading not required.)

1st Bn S Rifles

Instructions regarding War Diaries and Intelligence Summaries are contained in F. S. Regs., Part II. and the Staff Manual respectively. Title pages will be prepared in manuscript.

Place	Date	Hour	Summary of Events and Information	Remarks and references to Appendices
TRENCHES CUINCHY — LEFT SUBSECTION	March June 14.		A warm & sunny day, which cleared everybody up. The battalion by the 2nd R.W.F. & went back to billets in ANNEQUIN NORTH. We handed over the trenches in good condition & with all the safes dug out & their connecting trenches, we had also renetted part of them, COLDSTREAM LANE had been finally cleaned by this afternoon & made the relief easier. The following R.E. material was used by the battalion in the three days in trenches:— Sandbags 8500 Footboards 90 Plain wire 10 coils Quartering 110 ft. Nails 10 lbs. Wooden Pickets 20 Hurdles 30 (large & small)	

2353 Wt. W25144/1454 700,000 5/15 D. D. & L. A.D.S.S./Forms/C. 2118.

Army Form C. 2118.

WAR DIARY
or
INTELLIGENCE SUMMARY.

(Erase heading not required.)

1st S. Staffs

Instructions regarding War Diaries and Intelligence Summaries are contained in F.S. Regs., Part II. and the Staff Manual respectively. Title pages will be prepared in manuscript.

Place	Date	Hour	Summary of Events and Information	Remarks and references to Appendices
BILLETS ANNEQUIN NORTH	March Wed 15.		Greater part of the battalion on working parties in trenches. A draft of 27 men arrived for the battalion last night, under 2/Lieut J.A. Ritchie. Lieut C.D.P. Leighton also joined today.	
	Thurs 16.		The battalion was relieved at 4pm today by the 1st Bn MIDDLESEX REGT, & moved to billets in OBLINGHEM.	
OBLINGHEM	Fri 17.		Day was spent by the companies in kit, rifle etc. inspections. The billets are greatly improved since the last time we were in them; the sanitary arrangements, & billets generally have been put on a further footing & the men bedsteads have been erected in a certain number of billets.	
	Sat 18.		Company training. Particular attention is being paid to the drill & general smartness. Inter-company football league started in the afternoon.	
	Sun 19.		The companies in turn had the use of the baths in BETHUNE. Inter-company football in the afternoon.	

Army Form C. 2118.

WAR DIARY
or
INTELLIGENCE SUMMARY.

(Erase heading not required.)

1st S Rifles

Place	Date	Hour	Summary of Events and Information	Remarks and references to Appendices
BILLETS		March		
OBLINGHEM	Mon 30°		Companies training. The weather since we came here has been mild & fine, & have made it possible to use suitable fields for parades, as most of the mud has dried up.	
	Tues 31st		Companies training. The drill shows improvement already; it is so seldom that there is a chance of drilling units as large as a company, but here there is room.	
	Wed 22nd		Companies training. Weather is wet today. In the afternoon played to go & Royal Fusiliers in the Divisional Football Tournament.	
	Thurs 22nd		Companies training. We have added to the number & were told in the billets a have men but canvas over all those already erected.	
BEUVRY	Fri 2nd		Battalion marched at 11 am to billets in BEUVRY. The billets were good ones for both officers & men.	

Army Form C. 2118.

WAR DIARY
or
INTELLIGENCE SUMMARY.
(Erase heading not required.)

1st S Rifles

Instructions regarding War Diaries and Intelligence Summaries are contained in F. S. Regs., Part II. and the Staff Manual respectively. Title pages will be prepared in manuscript.

Place	Date	Hour	Summary of Events and Information	Remarks and references to Appendices
TRENCHES AUCHY LEFT SUB-SECTION	March Sat 25		Battalion went into trenches in the AUCHY (LEFT SUB-SECTION) relieving the 1st Bn THE QUEENS. The 4th Bn Suffolk Regt were on our left & the 5th Scottish Rifles on our right. The trenches were in good condition with the exception of the left company which was very bad indeed, both front line & breastwork.	
	Sun 26		All was quiet but there was a certain amount of rain which made the work in the left company trenches more slower than it would have been.	
	Mon 27		A quiet day, no shelling. A lot of work was got through on the left company & in the saps.	
	Tues 28		Still no shelling. The weather was bad, snow & rain.	
	Wed 29		All quiet. The battalion was relieved by the 2nd R.W.F. & marched back to billets in BEUVRY.	

Army Form C. 2118.

WAR DIARY
or
INTELLIGENCE SUMMARY.
(Erase heading not required.)

1st S. Rifles

Instructions regarding War Diaries and Intelligence Summaries are contained in F. S. Regs., Part II. and the Staff Manual respectively. Title pages will be prepared in manuscript.

Place	Date	Hour	Summary of Events and Information	Remarks and references to Appendices
BILLETS BEUVRY	March Thurs 30th		The battalion had the use of the baths. The billets were in good condition themselves but the ground near them was in a very bad state owing to the habits of the civilian inhabitants around certain billets.	
	Fri 31st		Companies carried out inspection of arms, clothing etc. A few working parties supplied for the trenches. "A" Company man was left by the battalion when it came out of trenches in WIMPOLE STREET & parties were supplied to a large extent from that company.	
	APRIL Sat 1st		Companies were employed in billets clearing up ground near them. Small working parties were supplied for trenches.	
	Sun 2nd		Battalion moved into trenches in AUCHY (LEFT SUB-SECTION) relieving the 2nd Bn. R.W.F. Trenches were dry, except in a few places.	

Army Form C. 2118.

WAR DIARY
or
INTELLIGENCE SUMMARY.
(Erase heading not required.)

Lt J Ryles

Instructions regarding War Diaries and Intelligence Summaries are contained in F. S. Regs., Part II. and the Staff Manual respectively. Title pages will be prepared in manuscript.

Place	Date	Hour	Summary of Events and Information	Remarks and references to Appendices
TRENCHES AUCHY LEFT SUB-SECTION	APRIL Mon 3rd		Work went on hard in the left company, which in places was beginning to assume a normal condition of repair. The enemy shelled the support line with field guns for a few minutes in the morning & from 4pm till about 6pm. No casualties & only small damage done to the trenches. Last night patrolling was done specially with a view to finding a suitable place for a raid against the enemy's trenches, however none was found & the enemy seems to sleep at points unsuited.	
	Tues 4th		Work continued as usual. Our Stokes guns were active & called forth heavy retaliation with field guns at various times during the day which stopped working parties for a time. Party night a great effort found that the selected spot for a raid was covered by wire of considerable depth in dead ground. They brought back a piece of the wire (?) were found on while cutting it, the enemy was on the alert. Lt. LAING led this patrol. During the day the enemy used a large proportion of phosphorus shells.	

2353 Wt. W2544/1454 700,000 5/15 D. D. & L. A.D.S.S./Forms/C. 2118.

WAR DIARY
or
INTELLIGENCE SUMMARY.

(Erase heading not required.)

Army Form C. 2118.

Lt J Ryles

Place	Date	Hour	Summary of Events and Information	Remarks and references to Appendices
TRENCHES AUCHY LEFT SUB-SECTION	APRIL 9th & 5th		The enemy shelled us with field guns intermittently throughout the day, chiefly in retaliation for our trench mortars which appear to cause considerable annoyance. LT. LAING took out a patrol at about 3.30 a.m. the morning & has taken up a position in a shell hole in the disused trench about 20 yds from the German parapet & he remained there all to-day. — LIEUT. LAING returned with his patrol to night having obtained valuable information regarding habits of enemy sentries, hour of standing to arms & method of carrying up rations, enemy snipers & machine guns. The patrol consisted of LIEUT. LAING, — CPL. TRIPP, — CPL. CAIRNS, — L/CPL. ROACH, — L/CPL. ROACH. (The patrol was afterwards complimented by the Army Commander & Divisional Commander.)	
	6th		The enemy again shelled us intermittently with field guns — in the early morning sent some rifle grenades into the front line of the night company. 7552 Pte W.T. OGILVIE was killed when out wiring last night. No. 10986 P/Cpl W. RAMSAY, 11991 Pte R. CONROY, 8126 Pte A. WHEELER were wounded. The battalion was relieved by the 2nd R.W.F. & marched back to billets in BEUVRY.	

Army Form C. 2118.

WAR DIARY
or
INTELLIGENCE SUMMARY.
(Erase heading not required.)

Instructions regarding War Diaries and Intelligence Summaries are contained in F. S. Regs., Part II. and the Staff Manual respectively. Title pages will be prepared in manuscript.

Place	Date April	Hour	Summary of Events and Information	Remarks and references to Appendices
BILLETS BEUVRY	Fri 2nd		The Companies were occupied with inspections. Small working parties were supplied for the trenches. Last night 'A' Company relieved a company of the 2/R.W.F. in WIMPOLE STREET.	
	Sat 8th		The battalion had the use of the baths in BEUVRY. The billets are good ones, but a good deal of work is being done to get the neighbouring ground cleaned of rubbish belonging to the inhabitants.	
	Sun 9th		The several denominations attended Divine Service.	
BETHUNE	Mon 10th		Battalion was relieved by the 4th Kings Regt & marched to billets in RUE D'AIRE. BETHUNE.	
	Tues 11th		Companies training & inspections. The weather is very unsettled.	
	Wed 12th		Companies had the use of the baths, & carried out drill parades & inspections. In the afternoon the first day of the Regtl Boxing Tournament took place.	

Army Form C. 2118.

WAR DIARY
or
INTELLIGENCE SUMMARY.
(Erase heading not required.)

1st J Ryl.

Place	Date	Hour	Summary of Events and Information	Remarks and references to Appendices
BILLETS BETHUNE	April Thurs 13th		Battalion paraded at 9.30 am for a Route March. One man fell out, the battalion as a whole marched well & march discipline was good. In the afternoon the semi-finals & finals of the Boxing Tournament took place, giving some very good fights.	
	Fri 14th		Companies carried out training & drill parades.	
	Sat 15th		Companies training. In the afternoon football match v. 2/R.W.F. was a win for the battalion 1-0.	
	Sun 16th		Divine Service for all denominations	
	Mon 17th		Companies carried out drill parades; we have been unable to find a piece of ground suitable for battalion parade.	

Army Form C. 2118.

WAR DIARY
or
INTELLIGENCE SUMMARY.
(Erase heading not required.)

1st of July 1914

Place	Date	Hour	Summary of Events and Information	Remarks and references to Appendices
BILLETS BETHUNE	April 18th		Greater part of day occupied with Training under Company arrangements and Musketry for Trenches. The Battalion started from Billets at 5.15 p.m. for Trenches. Guides from CUINCHY left antsection. Guides of the 1st Queens Regt were met at PONTFIXE and the relief completed well within 1½ hours. A dull day with drizzling rain. No 18768 Pte W. GOURLAY was wounded by enemy M.G. fire before entering communication trench during relief. Captain New did not go into trenches remaining with Transport tomorrow is going to duty in charge of Div School for Officers.	
TRENCHES CUINCHY Left subsec	Wed 19th		Weather stormy and cold. CO round Trenches in morning giving instructions to OCs Companies regarding work required to be done. Trenches officers both from evidence seen this morning and also last night, to have be left in good order by outgoing Regt. The following were wounded — Captain K. BUTTERFIELD, No 8738 Sergt A. WATSON, No B/8072 Pte T. JOHNSTON, No 16141 Pte J. MCNEALLY.	

WAR DIARY or INTELLIGENCE SUMMARY

Army Form C. 2118.

1st S. Buffs

Place	Date	Hour	Summary of Events and Information	Remarks and references to Appendices
TRENCHES CUINCHY Left subsec	April		Captain Butterfield's wound was serious though not dangerous as far as can be seen. Enemy M.G. fire were responsible. The order of Companies in trenches — which were not entered in yesterday's report is — Front line right A Coy, Centre D Coy, Left C Coy, Support B Coy.	
	Thurs 20th		Enemy sprung a mine at 4.45 a.m., making a crater some 30 yards across, covering its near lip 10 yards from our front line trench (occupied by A Coy) and No 10 ophead of our being destroyed, also part of adjoining sap blown in and our trenches a good deal shaken for some 70 yards round. Work was at once started clearing saps and other communications. This crater and adjoining crater being closely overlooked both from the German and our own observation Nests, no good object could be served by the actual occupation of near lip during daylight. Following were casualties — No 22470 Pte R. ADAMS an own	

Army Form C. 2118.

WAR DIARY
or
INTELLIGENCE SUMMARY.
(Erase heading not required.)

Lt L. Rifles

Place	Date	Hour	Summary of Events and Information	Remarks and references to Appendices
CUINCHY left subsec.	20th (continued)		Killed No 9114 L/Cpl W. BLOOMFIELD, No B/7175 H. WALKER, Wounded No 22470 Pte R. ADAMS, No 15810 Pte A. MOULTRIE, No 6860 Pte T. WARREN, No 18731 Pte W. SMITH, No 8303 L/Cpl J. WINSPER, No 18804 Pte G. ROWLAND, No A/7663 Pte A. McLAREN. Above casualties were in connection with mine. Also wounded by shell fire in communication trench same evening No 7077 J. STEVENSON and No 8401 Pte M. CULLEN. A raid on two enemy saps was carried out at 9.30 p.m. with cooperation of Trench Mortars and Artillery. Lieuts MUNRO and PERCY each led 15 men. The enemy saps were found to have been evacuated with the exception of 1 man with whom Lieut PERCY had an encounter at close quarters, the German unfortunately escaping.	
	Fri 21st		A considerable amount of ammunition today, but trenches have become very water-logged. Steady work of repairing and draining is being put in on them. In the evening a patrol went out	

Army Form C. 2118.

WAR DIARY
or
INTELLIGENCE SUMMARY.
(Erase heading not required.)

1st / Rifles

Instructions regarding War Diaries and Intelligence Summaries are contained in F. S. Regs., Part II. and the Staff Manual respectively. Title pages will be prepared in manuscript.

Place	Date	Hour	Summary of Events and Information	Remarks and references to Appendices
TRENCHES CUINCHY and Left subsection	April 1 & 2 2nd		from D Company under Capt. Brickman who was accompanied by Lieut Ritchie. It gave an enemy wire was taken advantage of with the object of nobbling a sentry, but the enemy were alert and a hand grenade thrown at the party went very near Lieut Ritchie. Our patrol then retired after getting soaked to the skin, the weather having again become squally. Weather cold and rainy again. Company worked hard to put trenches into as good order as possible. 20th Royal Fusiliers who relieved us, stating to 7 P.M. Relief completed in 2 hours. Most of our casualties during this Tour in Trenches were the result of the enemy mine explosion. The Enemy have refrained from any real retaliation either at the time or on days following the expedition of our Patrols against their Trenches. We moved into billets at LE QUESNOY.	

Army Form C. 2118.

WAR DIARY
or
INTELLIGENCE SUMMARY.
(Erase heading not required.)

1st L Rifles

Place	Date	Hour	Summary of Events and Information	Remarks and references to Appendices
BILLETS LE QUESNOY	April Sun 23rd		Easter Day. Divine Service were voluntary. B and C Companies were employed on work of cleaning trenches near front line, remainder of Battn to clean themselves and construction of additional incinerators, Baths &c round billets. Billets were left very clean on the whole by 20th R Fusiliers	
	Mon 24th		A and D Companies went to front line trenches for work.	
	Tues 25th		B and C Companies went to front line trenches for work.	
	Wed 26th		The Battalion relieved the 20th Royal Fusiliers in Curluy left sub-section, (many PONTFIXE at 7 p.m. Relief took 2½ hours, being slower than before owing to extra long distances being ordered between parties on march to trenches. The Germans have been rather free with their artillery the last day or two. Companies took the	

Army Form C. 2118.

WAR DIARY
or
INTELLIGENCE SUMMARY.

(Erase heading not required.)

1st L Rifles

Instructions regarding War Diaries and Intelligence Summaries are contained in F. S. Regs., Part II. and the Staff Manual respectively. Title pages will be prepared in manuscript.

Place	Date	Hour	Summary of Events and Information	Remarks and references to Appendices
	April 26th (cont)		following positions - C Coy right, B Coy centre, D Coy left, A Coy Support. Enemy appear very much on the alert and apprehensive. A good deal of traversing M.G. fire upon our front line and some enemy during night. Casualties are one killed in Armd listening Post by 17.G. fire, No 6730 Pte W.VALLANCE.	
TRENCHES CUINCHY left sub-section	June 27th		A big Artillery bombardment heard to commence at 5.15.a.m. to south of us. Turned out to be a German Gas attack on LOOS salient. The Battalion received orders from Bde H.Q. at 9 a.m. to look out for gas and men in forward area put on helmets in their sheds. No gas felt by us though it affected people at Bde H.Q. LE PRÉOL and in BEUVRY. During morning enemy lights artillery were active, chiefly directed on CUINCHY Church. S/Lt Chaplin went to Brigade H.Q. to command during absence of Brigadier in Leave. Lieut Duncan left Trenches to go to 1st Army Instructional School.	

WAR DIARY
or
INTELLIGENCE SUMMARY.

Army Form C. 2118.

Place	Date	Hour	Summary of Events and Information	Remarks and references to Appendices
as Adjt and 2nd Lieuts	April Tues 28th		Enemy sniped and fired M.Gs again during night, also fired some rifle grenades. Shelling by Enemy of CUINCHY village & during morning otherwise quiet during day. One casualty No 9836 Pte J. Macey was wounded by rifle grenade. At 8.15 p.m. gas gongs were heard sounding in Brigade just north of us and the alarm was taken up by our left Company and passed back to Batt H.Q. and other Companies. Artillery were also notified. All ranks were inside their gas helmets in a very few seconds. No gas came along and it was not discovered what had started the alarm in the Brigade to north of us. Many of our men were quite disappointed that the Enemy did not come over his parapet.	
	Wed 29th		A sharp bombardment heard to south of us at 4.15 a.m. again	

WAR DIARY
or
INTELLIGENCE SUMMARY.
(Erase heading not required.)

Army Form C. 2118.

1st S. Staffs

Place	Date	Hour	Summary of Events and Information	Remarks and references to Appendices
	April 29th	(a)	Turned out to be a fruitless effort of the Enemy opposite LOOS. Quiet during remainder of day until 10 p.m. when a bombardment of enemy's trenches to our right front by our Artillery and Trench Mortars took place. This called forth considerable retaliation by enemy's guns directed on CUINCHY village and trenches in line with it but harmless in result to our personnel. Coy Sergt Major Frankham was badly wounded by the explosion of a rifle grenade which he was putting into a rifle.	
	April 30th		A comparatively quiet day, but between 5 and 7 p.m. Enemy dropped a few H.E. shells in our trenches. No casualties from this to our men, but a man of the R.W.F. on a Mining working party had his head blown off. Relief by the 2nd Bn Royal Fusiliers commenced about 7.30 p.m. and was completed in an hour and a half. Weather has been fine throughout these 4 days and a great deal of	

Army Form C. 2118.

1st S Rifles

WAR DIARY
or
INTELLIGENCE SUMMARY.
(Erase heading not required.)

Instructions regarding War Diaries and Intelligence Summaries are contained in F. S. Regs., Part II. and the Staff Manual respectively. Title pages will be prepared in manuscript.

Place	Date	Hour	Summary of Events and Information	Remarks and references to Appendices
	April 30th (cont)		has been done, mostly in building up and revetting damaged fire trenches. Working parties of the 20th Royal Fus came up night and day, at night to help with putting up wire. The men of the 20th R.F. require a great amount of supervision and instruction in the particular, having little notion of wiring. They are a "Public School" Battalion and very well educated and excellent in many respects. The Battalion (min brn) went back to billets at LE QUESNOY. F.A.C. Hamilton Cmdg 1st Batt Rifle Cameronians	

WAR DIARY 1/13 7th Common... 1 Scottish Rgt.
INTELLIGENCE SUMMARY.

Army Form C. 2118

Place	Date	Hour	Summary of Events and Information	Remarks and references to Appendices
	April 30th (cont)		has been done, mostly in building up and revetting damaged fire trenches. Working parties of the 20th Royal Fus. came up nightly and day, at night to help with putting up wire. The men of the 20th R.F. require a great amount of supervision and instruction in this particular, having little notion of wiring. They are a "Public Schools" Battalion and very well educated and excellent in many respects. The Battalion (our own) went back to billets at LE QUESNOY. Last month already #####	
BILLETS May 1st LE QUESNOY	May 1st		A & D Companies to firstline trenches for work; remainder engaged cleaning up and drill under Company arrangements. A draft of 17 NCOs and Men was inspected, having arrived from Base Depot previous day. Half of them had been out before with 2nd and 9th (Service) Battalion. Sergt Major Frankham died in Hospital. He was a good soldier.	

WAR DIARY
or
INTELLIGENCE SUMMARY.

Army Form C. 2118.

Place	Date	Hour	Summary of Events and Information	Remarks and references to Appendices
	May Tues 2nd		B & C Companies to work in front line trenches. Funeral of Coy. S.M. Frankham in afternoon at BETHUNE Cemetery.	
	Wed 3rd		A & D Companies to work in front line trenches. Inspection of Regt. Transport by C.O.	
	Thurs 4th		The 19th Brigade went into Div Reserve. The Battalion moved back to ANNEZIN, taking over billets from the 4th (Territorial) Battn Suffolk Regt. Billets fairly clean but not calculated to hold more than 500 men and we are nearly 800.	
Billets in ANNEZIN	Fri 5th		Companies occupied cleaning kit and billets. Kit of all Companies laid out and inspected by Commanding Officer. Kits good on the whole, but one Company which had had many changes in its Commanders showed itself deficient of a good many shirts and socks, 2 shirts and 3 pairs socks being	

WAR DIARY
or
INTELLIGENCE SUMMARY.

(Erase heading not required.)

Army Form C. 2118.

Place	Date	Hour	Summary of Events and Information	Remarks and references to Appendices
	May 5 (contd)		the minimum required by under regimental arrangements. Tents were obtained from Brigade to supplement billeting accommodation.	
	Sat 6		Battalion paraded as strong as possible in Marching Order. Turn-out was creditable on the whole and Officers commanding Platoons showed a realization of their responsibilities in connection with clothing and equipment of their men in most cases.	
	Sun 7		Church Parades for Presbyterian Church of Scotland, C of E, & R.C. The C.O. conducted an outdoor tactical exercise for the 2 senior officers in each company and bombing and Lewis gun officers in the afternoon. The G.O.C. 33rd Div. paid the Battalion a visit at midday and inspected dinners. He made a point of even being more used with a view to greater variety of diet.	
	Mon 8		Baths were allotted for all Companies. 2 Companies were	

WAR DIARY or INTELLIGENCE SUMMARY

Place	Date	Hour	Summary of Events and Information	Remarks and references to Appendices
	May 6th (cont)		exercised in fire discipline and bayonet fighting and 2 coys attended a Brigade tactical exercise. Half the Officers and N.C.O's in each Company marched forward to study the Reserve lines of Defence behind the 23rd Div front.	
	Tues 9th		Companies carried out Training as on 8th. Forms of Company training with transports in each other. The other half of Officers and NCOs visited Reserve line. 2/Lt Chaplin proceeded on leave.	
	Wed 10th		Brigade route march of 9 miles was carried out. Battalion as usual and first-line transport. The Battalion turn-out showed 693 ORs, Mules out of 770. Turn-outs was good. Men had worked to clean their web-equipment, rifles and were out to make the most of their clothing and equipment generally; also horses and vehicles of transport were good. The G.O.C Division May[?]	

Place	Date	Hour	Summary of Events and Information	Remarks and references to Appendices
	May 10th (cont)		Major General London, expressed himself through the G.O.C. Brigade as being very pleased with the turn out of the Brigade and particularly of the Ceremonial. No men fell out. A Brigade Boxing Tournament took place in the afternoon at BETHUNE. We won two finals, in Middle and Light weights.	
	Thurs 11th		Companies exercised in rapid loading and firing and drill.	
	Fri 12th		2 Companies practiced an movements while wearing gas helmets and fire discipline, 2 companies in bayonet fighting and company drill.	
	Sat 13th		Weather which had been fine, if cold for time of year, broke and rain prevented the Carrying out C.O's Parade as arranged. Training under Company arrangements were carried out. Final Company football tie was played. It was the	

Army Form C. 2118.

WAR DIARY
or
INTELLIGENCE SUMMARY.
(Erase heading not required.)

Instructions regarding War Diaries and Intelligence Summaries are contained in F. S. Regs., Part II. and the Staff Manual respectively. Title pages will be prepared in manuscript.

Place	Date	Hour	Summary of Events and Information	Remarks and references to Appendices
	May 13th	(con)	afternoon between B and C Companies, C Coy winning.	
	June 14th		Church Parade for all Denominations.	
	May 15th		Companies carried out Training as on 12th inst, parties of Companies changing over subjects.	
	June 16th		The Battalion left ANNEZIN. Out of 12 days weather has only interfered with Training on 2 days. Besides Training carried out all Platoons have carried out running practice before breakfasts. 130 Men have been recently inoculated & must return while in their billets. The Battalion marched to ANNEQUIN South and took over billets from our own 6th (Territorial) Battalion.	

WAR DIARY
or
INTELLIGENCE SUMMARY.
(Erase heading not required.)

Army Form C. 2118.

Place	Date	Hour	Summary of Events and Information	Remarks and references to Appendices
Billet at ANNEQUIN South	May Wed 17th		The chief work consists here in furnishing working parties to the front trenches, mostly tunnelling shifts of 8 hours. With one company kept as a Reserve the other 3 Companies find it all they can do to find the Men required. Inspection of billets and of trenches and dug-outs for cover from any artillery bombardment was carried out by C.O. A good many shells fell about 200 yards wide on either side of the road, thereby which we are billeted about 7.30 p.m., the Enemy evidently searching for our artillery. An enemy aeroplane hovered about some 200 yards from battalion H.Q. billet in the evening	
	Thurs 18th		All available men employed in working parties near front trenches. 1st Col Chaplin returned from leave.	
	Fri 19th		Battn at ANNEQUIN North allotted to the Battalion were taken	

Place	Date	Hour	Summary of Events and Information	Remarks and references to Appendices
	May		advantage of by sandwiching visits to Battn in between the working party shifts.	
	31st 20th		C.O. visited shelter trenches round billets to see how cover and accommodation was being improved. Companies are keeping 6 inches and shovels at work for 2 hours each day in this. Some of the officers played cricket in the afternoon, one ball available, pick handle for bat, and ration box for wickets. We carry footballs for the Men's use.	
	June 21st		Uneventful except for an invasion of our billeting area by lachrymatory gas about 7 p.m. It was strong enough to make everyone's eyes water and smart. The goggles in possession are not much use. The gas is believed to have come from shells burst (enemy's) somewhere near SOUCHEZ 10 miles off.	

WAR DIARY
or
INTELLIGENCE SUMMARY.
(Erase heading not required.)

Army Form C. 2118.

Place	Date	Hour	Summary of Events and Information	Remarks and references to Appendices
	May Mon 22ⁿᵈ		We are leaving our billets the better for the addition by our Pioneers of 2 skeleton trenches, improvements generally to latrines, and extension of shelter trenches. The Battalion relieved the 20ᵗʰ Royal Fusiliers in trenches, AUCHY Left sub-section, guides meeting our parties at 9.30 p.m. Relief was completed by 11.30 p.m. No casualties.	
Trenches AUCHY Left sub-sec	Tues 23ʳᵈ		Trenches clean, but lots of work wanting to be done on some of them, and sentry duties in pretty heavy. Companies are disposed from right to left D, B, A with C in Reserve. About 3 a.m. a German put up his head in a forward sap and said "good morning." He also threw over a message to say they were tired of the War and did not care who won. Sniping continued from both sides, and the German disappeared. Our Artillery in co-operation with Trench mortars bombarded enemy's front system in the afternoon and again at 10.30 p.m.	

Place	Date	Hour	Summary of Events and Information	Remarks and references to Appendices
	May 23rd (cont)		Enemy Trenches appear to be badly knocked about. Retaliation by their artillery and rifle grenades resulted in five casualties to the Battalion, all wounded, No 11146 L/Cpl P. Winter, No 9326 Pte E. Ellis, No 8073 Pte H. Slavin, No 10996 Pte K. Hynds, No 6663 Pte J. Thompson. Our snipers claim two casualties.	
	Wed 24th		Our Artillery carried out further bombardments of enemy's front system, into the part which has just clear of our left, at 12.15 a.m. and 2.15 a.m., & the latter hour brings back some retaliation. Between these hours B Company "stood to" to watch for any movement when the German of last night had shown himself. Instructions had been received from Div HQrs that any party trying to desert from the Enemy might be to be allowed in. Nothing of the sort happened. At 8 P.m. enemy artillery and minenwerfer bombarded the sub-section immediately north of us. Our left Company's trenches came in for some of it but we had no casualties.	

WAR DIARY
or
INTELLIGENCE SUMMARY.

(Erase heading not required.)

Army Form C. 2118.

Place	Date	Hour	Summary of Events and Information	Remarks and references to Appendices
	May Thurs 25th		Enemy quiet except for some artillery return on both sides and usual exchange of hand grenades from saps.	
	Fri 26th		A normal day in trenches. Arrangements were made during the evening for measures to be taken in connection with the blowing of a new crater by the Mining Company on our front.	
	Sat 27th	1 a.m.	At 1 a.m. land mines which had been placed by our Miners round Queens Crater were exploded. We had at the same time this Crater, and at 2 a.m. our Grenadiers started throwing bombs from the crater with the object of driving the Germans out into the far lip. Some bombs were thrown back at our men so it is hoped that a good few Germans were up against the far lip of Queens Crater when after our Grenadiers had retired, 2600 lbs of ammonal was exploded close to the Crater, forming a new and larger one in which the original Queens Crater	

WAR DIARY
or
INTELLIGENCE SUMMARY.

(Erase heading not required.)

Army Form C. 2118.

Place	Date	Hour	Summary of Events and Information	Remarks and references to Appendices
	May 27th (cont)		was engulfed. Enemy Artillery opened fire but we suffered no casualties. Our men were busy during the day digging out the saps and sap-heads and adjusting their position to the enlarged crater. Germans put over some rifle grenades and a few minenwerfer without causing us casualties. We were relieved in the evening at 8.36 p.m by the 20th Royal Fusiliers and went into billets at ANNEZIN-S ANNEQUIN. South	
Billets ANNEZIN South	June 28th		Billets we found left clean and fairly tidy by the 20th R.F. Refuse have to be buried without burning here as incinerators are not allowed owing to closeness of the front line. Enemy artillery was rather active in the vicinity and in the evening some half dozen shrapnel were burst quite close to our billets without causing damage. The battalion was to have moved back to BEUVRY but orders were issued that all battalions were to stand fast. The 98th Brigade on our	

Army Form C. 2118.

WAR DIARY
or
INTELLIGENCE SUMMARY.
(Erase heading not required.)

Place	Date	Hour	Summary of Events and Information	Remarks and references to Appendices
	May 28th (cont)		left were being unexpectedly retaken out of trenches and being relieved by the Reserve Brigade of the 39th Division. Intelligence points to an expected enemy offensive not far from our front.	
	Mon 29th		Enemy indulged in intermittent shelling of the support line trenches in our front and also searched for our artillery. The Battalion moved back to BEUVRY in the evening to billets vacated by the 2nd Royal Welsh Fusiliers.	
	Tues 30th		Though 3 miles behind trenches we had to furnish over 200 N.C.O's and Men during the day to work on and near front trenches. The Men had little rest last tour of trenches and every man was on a working party every day while at ANNEQUIN. But they keep fit and cheerful. Cleaning billets and clothes occupied those not on working parties.	

WAR DIARY
or
INTELLIGENCE SUMMARY.

Place	Date	Hour	Summary of Events and Information	Remarks and references to Appendices
	May Wed 31st		A draft 122 strong arrived as a reinforcement to the Battalion from the 6th (Territorial) Batts Scottish Rifles. Also a draft of 50 rank and file arrived from the Base Depot. They were played in by our Pipers. The strength of the Battalion is now made up to 1106. Working parties only amounted to 120 today.	

Malcolm
Lt. Col.
Comdg 1st Bn. The Cameronians

SECRET.

D.A.G.
 General Headquarters.
  3rd Echelon.
   Base.
....

A "Certified true Copy" of the Duplicate War Diary for the month of June 1916 is forwarded herewith.

The original copy was forwarded to you on or about the 2nd July 1916, and apparently has miscarried in the post.

1916.   Lieut Colonel,
          Commanding, 1stBn: The Cameronians.

WAR DIARY
or
INTELLIGENCE SUMMARY
(Erase heading not required.)

Army Form C. 2118.
33 1 Scottish Rifles JUNE
Vol 23
19.M. 11 weeks

Place	Date	Hour	Summary of Events and Information	Remarks and references to Appendices
Billets BEUVRY	June Thurs 1st		Practically no working parties to-day, these being furnished by the 2/5th Royal Warwicks of the 61st Div. first arrived in the country. We loaned them guides and steel helmets. Beyond cleaning themselves and kits, and routine inspections of articles of equipment etc, the men were given a rest.	
	Fri. 2nd.		The Battalion left BEUVRY at 7-30 p.m. and moved into trenches, relieving the 20th Royal Fusiliers in AUCHY left sub-section. Disposition of companies was — front-line right-to-left C, B, A — Support D. One Company of the 2/5th Warwicks came in trenches with us for instruction and was attached to C. Coy. No Casualties.	
Trenches AUCHY-left	Sat. 3rd.		A few light T. Mortar bombs and rifle grenades were fired into A Company's trenches and part of B's during the day. We had three casualties No 7811 Pte D. COLMAN and No 16749 Pte W.M. COOMBES both of A Coy and No 9367 Pte T. NIXON B. Coy. Our Artillery and trench mortars are	

WAR DIARY
or
INTELLIGENCE SUMMARY
(Erase heading not required.)

Army Form C. 2118.

Place	Date	Hour	Summary of Events and Information	Remarks and references to Appendices
Trenches AUCHY-left	June		doing some steady and not too obtrusive work cutting the German wire opposite QUEENS Crater.	
	Sun 4th		The 121 Men of the bd. Scottish Rifles who have only been with us 4 days were marched off for return to their Regiment which is not being disbanded as apparently had been intended. More wire cutting by our artillery and T. Mortars and brisk retaliation from the Enemy. 2 Artillerymen in our trenches casualties from shelling, 1 killed. No casualties to us during daylight. At 11 p.m. a Raiding Party formed by D Company augmented with E Coy's bombers crossed No-mans Land from QUEENS crater into the German front line trench and returned with one prisoner having killed 6. Our advance was covered by Artillery and T. Mortars. Captain D. Evans was in command. Lieut. R.B. Ritchie shot two of the Germans	

Army Form C. 2118.

WAR DIARY
or
INTELLIGENCE SUMMARY

(Erase heading not required.)

Instructions regarding War Diaries and Intelligence Summaries are contained in F. S. Regs., Part II. and the Staff Manual respectively. Title Pages will be prepared in manuscript.

Place	Date	Hour	Summary of Events and Information	Remarks and references to Appendices
Trenches AUCHY-Left	June		with his revolver and was instrumental in saving the one prisoner brought in alive. Our casualties were 5 wounded and 1 missing: wounded:- No. 7579 L.C/Sr J. KERR, No 7921 L.C/Sr J. McINTOSH, No. 18751 R H R. CRAUFORD, No. 8603 R H R. NEEDHAM all of D. Coy and No. 17644 R H J. GEDDES of C. Coy. Telegrams of congratulation were received from Army Commander, Divisional Commander and G.O.C. Brigade.	
	Mon 5th		A heavy bombardment of the trenches occupied by our left Company and the trenches immediately North of us, in retaliation for last nights raid, between 5 and 6 a.m. We sustained no casualties. After this a quiet day but several bomb throwing after dark when two men were wounded, No 11159 R H M. RAFFERTY, and No 8969 Pte A. KELLY both of A. Coy. The G.O.C. Division visited Battalion Hd. Qrs to hear about the raid as also did the G.O.C. Brigade. Captain Evans and Lieut. Ritchie were taken back to BETHUNE to tell the Army Commander and other of the General Staff all about it.	

Army Form C. 2118.

WAR DIARY
or
INTELLIGENCE SUMMARY

(Erase heading not required.)

Place	Date	Hour	Summary of Events and Information	Remarks and references to Appendices
Trenches AUCHY. Left.	June 6th.		A normal day in the trenches — We had no casualties.	
	Wed 7th.		A fairly quiet day with occasional bursts of light ar'tillery and T.Mortars on both sides. We had one man killed through looking over the top of a crater lip instead of using the periscope — No 9244 Pte G. GASON, B Company.	
	Thur 8th.		Some kind of day as the 7th until 4-30 p.m when an underground gallery was blown close to QUEENS crater covered by fire from our Artillery and T.Mortars. Enemy retaliated in kind causing 2 casualties in a party from a Pioneer Battalion. One Company of the 2/6th Warwicks Regt. joined us in Trenches and took over our right Company's Front-line, being left with 1 N.C.O. per Platoon and 1 Officer of our right (c) Company to help them, as they are new to trench work.	

Place	Date	Hour	Summary of Events and Information	Remarks and references to Appendices
	Fri 9th June		A quiet day. The Battalion was relieved by the 16th K.R.R. of the 100th Brigade. Our Companies marched back to billets in ANNEZIN, 6 miles, packs being carried in wagons.	
BILLETS ANNEZIN	Sat 10th		The day was given up to settling into billets and cleaning clothing and equipment. The men are very fit but need their rest after 24 days spent either actually occupying trenches or supplying working parties for them. Billets have been left clean by the Glasgow Highlanders	
	Sun 11th		Church parade for all denominations. Two platoons of D. Coy. and 10 bombers of C. Coy. who took part in the raid of June 4th were paraded before Major General Landon Comdg. the Division who addressed them in congratulatory terms	
	Mon 12th		The day was occupied with inspections of clothing, equipment etc by O.C's companies. A party of officers and other	

WAR DIARY
or
INTELLIGENCE SUMMARY

(Erase heading not required.)

Army Form C. 2118.

Place	Date	Hour	Summary of Events and Information	Remarks and references to Appendices
Billets ANNEZIN	June Mon 12th.		ranks was sent to undergo the experience of being put through a chamber filled with gas - with their helmets on.	
	13th.			
	14th. 15th.		The usual programme of training in billets was carried out.	
	16th.		The pipers and buglers of the Battn. took part in a Brigade Tattoo in the square in BETHUNE. The Battn. gave a concert in the evening.	
	Sat 17th.	10pm	Inspection by the Corps Commander who expressed himself highly pleased with the turnout and general smart appearance of the Battn. The Battn. paraded in Mass at nearly full strength.	
		4pm	Marched to LE QUESNOY and went into billets there.	
Billets LE QUESNOY	Sun 18th.		Church Parades.	
	Mon 19th.		C.O. and Company Commanders went up to look at trenches etc. which the Battn. will occupy in the VILLAGE LINE	

Army Form C. 2118.

WAR DIARY
or
INTELLIGENCE SUMMARY
(Erase heading not required.)

Place	Date	Hour	Summary of Events and Information	Remarks and references to Appendices
VILLAGE LINE GIVENCHY	June 20th	9 p.m.	Battn. relieved the 2nd A. & S. Highlanders in VILLAGE LINE forming Support to GIVENCHY SECTOR. The front line was held by 2/R.Welsh Fusiliers on Left and 20th ROYAL FUSILIERS on right. Companies started up the LA BASSÉE CANAL by Platoons at 100yd intervals but owing to shelling were compelled to make a detour which delayed the relief.	
	Wed 21st.		A quiet day. GIVENCHY KEEP was shelled about 1 p.m. Companies started work on the various keeps in VILLAGE LINE which were found to be in a bad state of repair.	
	Thurs 22nd	2 A.M.	Enemy blew a large mine near DUCK'S BILL and shelled front, support and reserve lines for 1½ hours. He then made a raid which was repulsed by 2/Royal Welsh Fusiliers. One Company of the R.W.F. suffered severely losing about 150 men. This Company was withdrawn and replaced by our A Company about 10 A.M. We lost a few men by shell fire	
			Casualties:- Killed: No 22199 Pte. G. FARREN D Coy.	
			Wounded:- 16986 Pte I. PERCY - No 25544 t/c HALL, 17294 Pte. THOMPSON	
			A Coy - 4 No. 13292 Pte McINALLY - A. Coy.	
			D - 1	

WAR DIARY
or
INTELLIGENCE SUMMARY
(Erase heading not required.)

Army Form C. 2118.

Place	Date	Hour	Summary of Events and Information	Remarks and references to Appendices
VILLAGE LINE GIVENCHY	June Fri. 23rd		Quiet day. A lot of work done on keeps etc. CASUALTIES:- No. 18715 Pte D. MACKAY - A. Coy - wounded. No 21375 L/c HUGHES. No. 25799 Rg ANDREWS - A Coy. wounded both the latter by a rifle grenade.	
	Sat. 24th		Our guns shelled selected points in the German Lines at intervals during the day. This led to some retaliation. Killed. - No 11285 Pte I. WHITE - A. Coy. Wounded - No 7147 L/c C. EDGELL, No. 8618 Pte. R. LIVINGSTONE. No A7117 Pte I. HOWIE, No 18767 " I. FURNESS No 10909 " I. BLYTH, ― A Company. A. Coy - 5.	
	Sun 25th		The floor of GIVENCHY KEEP fell in, precipitating 4 men into a cess pool from which they were rescued with difficulty. INJURED No 22354 Pte F. WINTERS, No 22236 Pte W. GREENLEES, D-Coy. No 22375 " W. ROSS , No 6023 " D. SEENAN	

Army Form C. 2118.

WAR DIARY
or
INTELLIGENCE SUMMARY
(Erase heading not required.)

Instructions regarding War Diaries and Intelligence Summaries are contained in F.S. Regs., Part II. and the Staff Manual respectively. Title Pages will be prepared in manuscript.

Place	Date	Hour	Summary of Events and Information	Remarks and references to Appendices
Trenches Right Sector GIVENCHY.	June Mon 26th	9 P.M.	The Bn. relieved the 20th Royal Fusiliers in the Front line Trenches astride the LA BASSÉE CANAL. C + D. Companies took over N. of the Canal A + B Companies South of it. The trenches N. of the Canal and CHEYNE WALK were in a bad state of repair.	
	Tues 27th		Our Artillery shelled the Germans but provoked practically no reply. CASUALTIES:- WOUNDED:- No 6836 CPL BRUNTON - B. Coy. No 22294 PTE THOMPSON D. Coy 3 No 25547 PTE MULLINS No. 19779 PTE SAUNDERS - D. Coy. B. Coy 2	
	Wed 28th		A number of mines blown in the vicinity, (in all but none on our immediate front. A quiet day. WOUNDED No 7979 PTE OLIVER B. Coy. B. Coy 1.	
	Thurs 29th		Heavy shelling about dusk near MADPOINT, at about 10 P.M the Enemy shelled our front line for a short time just S. of the Canal CASUALTIES: KILLED. 2/Lt. T.R. BROWNLIE - No 9941 PTE JOHNSTONE - D. Coy. WOUNDED. No. 12510 L/c. HULME - D Coy. No 22643 - PTE WATSON - D Coy No 11165 PTE BAKEWELL - B. Coy. No 13007 - OSBORNE - B Coy	

Army Form C. 2118.

WAR DIARY
or
INTELLIGENCE SUMMARY

(Erase heading not required.)

Place	Date	Hour	Summary of Events and Information	Remarks and references to Appendices
Trenches R. Sector. GIVENCHY	June Fri. 30th		Trenches nearly dry after recent rain. Companies worked on thickening parapets, carrying platoon on CHEYNE WALK. Some Ninemenfire fired. One on brickstacks at night.	

Signed J.G. Chaplin Lt. Col.
Comdg. the Cameronians.

Certified true copy.

Lieut. Colonel.
Commanding 1st Battalion The Cameronians.

19th Inf.Bde.
33rd Div.

WAR DIARY

1st BATTN. THE CAMERONIANS (SCOTTISH RIFLES).

J U L Y

1 9 1 6

WAR DIARY
or
INTELLIGENCE SUMMARY.

(Erase heading not required.)

Army Form C. 2118.

Place	Date	Hour	Summary of Events and Information	Remarks and references to Appendices
Ayth Sucks S.E.	July 1st		Received news of the start of offensive on the SOMME. Our artillery continued to bombard enemy's lines. Retaliation feeble. Casualty: - Killed by a stray bullet - No 9252 C.Q.M.S. HEMMINGS B Coy	
TRENCHY	2nd		Quiet day. The Battn. was relieved by 2nd R. Fusiliers and went back to Brigade Support in Village Line. A mine was exploded on our right which shook the dug out but caused two men. Casualties:- KILLED No 11275 Pte DOHERTY - No Pte PIGG - D Coy	
VILLAGE LINE	3rd 4th		two front line posts, men rested and cleaned their rifles & bombing.	
			Work on defenses. Casualties - wounded, 10326 Pte STEWART C. Coy 1/7/16	
			Pte CROCKFORD D Coy 2/7/16	
	5th		WELCH FUSILIERS made a most successful raid on the German trenches opposite, a certain amount of shells came over in consequence but no damage done.	
LE PREOL	6th		The Battn. moved back to huts in LE PREOL in the evening, Orders arrived later to be ready to move tomorrow night, destination unknown	

WAR DIARY
or
INTELLIGENCE SUMMARY.
(Erase heading not required.)

Army Form C. 2118.

Instructions regarding War Diaries and Intelligence Summaries are contained in F.S. Regs., Part II. and the Staff Manual respectively. Title pages will be prepared in manuscript.

Place	Date	Hour	Summary of Events and Information	Remarks and references to Appendices
LE PRÉOL	July Fri. 7/15		The Batt. paraded by Coys. at 11 P.M. and marched to OBLINGHEM (7 kilometres). A by relieved us & we entrained at 5.30 A.M.	
OBLINGHEM	Sat. 8/15	12.30p	The Batt. marched to FOUQUEREUIL entrainment (3 miles) and entrained. Arrived at AMIENS about 9.30 p.m. and detrained at LONGUEAU. Left for a station at 11 p.m. and marched to POULAINVILLE arriving there at 2 A.M. (about 8 miles)	
POULAINVILLE	Sun 9/15		The men were very tired, it was a hot march but kept up wonderfully fine.	
	Mon 10/15		Remained in billets. Orders to march at 4 P.M. but cancelled at last moment.	
DAOURS	Tues 11/15	5.45AM	marched with rest of Brigade to DAOURS (7½ miles) and went into billets. Packs hauled into store in the evening.	
BUIRE	12/15 13/15		marched in the afternoon to BUIRE and billeted there. Remained in billets next day to move on to have baths.	
MEAULTE	14/15		Paraded at 10 A.M. & marched to MEAULTE went into billets (for 2 hours) paraded again at 2 P.M. & marched 2 miles and then bivouacked in a field for the night. 3 shells fell amongst "A" Batt.	

WAR DIARY or INTELLIGENCE SUMMARY

Army Form C. 2118.

Place	Date	Hour	Summary of Events and Information	Remarks and references to Appendices
MAMETZ WOOD	July Sat 15th	9.8 am – 4.0 pm	Paraded 4 A.M. & marched to MAMETZ WOOD to be in reserve to an attack made by 98th Brigade. Lady Pilrus all day anticipating orders. Lt. Col. Chaplin was out with the R.S.O. being left not in reserve brigade. The Regt was much worried by Ten shells during the night.	
HIGH WOOD	Sun 16th		At 1 A.M. received orders to file in on the line near HIGH WOOD. The Bns marched up at 11.20 A.M. and got into position before daylight, relieving & machine up 9th 2 no Highlanders and other regiments. C company lost by sniping & T.M. & Machine gun fire quite heavily. D walked into a German Machine gun on the edge of the wood & had several casualties. Capt GOULDEN — 2Lt CHARLTON killed — 2Lt WATSON & other ranks killed 2 — wounded 46. In the afternoon the Bn was withdrawn & went into trenches near BAZENTIN-LE-PETIT. Moved again in the night. No stop for any sleep.	

Army Form C. 2118.

WAR DIARY
or
INTELLIGENCE SUMMARY.
(Erase heading not required.)

Instructions regarding War Diaries and Intelligence Summaries are contained in F. S. Regs., Part II. and the Staff Manual respectively. Title pages will be prepared in manuscript.

Place	Date	Hour	Summary of Events and Information	Remarks and references to Appendices
BAZENTIN	17		Ordered to attack German Switch Trench. Remained S. of BAZENTIN LE-PETIT in most intermittent cover, heavy shelling. Attack postponed 24 hours. Casualties minimal - Pte Barclay 196th killed.	
	Tues 18		Shelling continued. Suspension moved to 4.U. In position at 2 am very ready for assault. Attack again postponed. Casualties killed 1 wounded - 32	
	Wed 19		Moved from the trenches on edge of MAMETZ WOOD. at 7 P.M. Received news at 10 p.m. had to attack HIGH WOOD at dawn. Arrived at position of assembly at 12 midnight. No sleep. Rain started. In position in HIGH WOOD at 2 A.M. heavy Trench Mortar batteries barrage. 5th Sea. Rifles were near Pyle	
HIGH WOOD	20		1.30 guns when over of battery barrage. Went into the wood. At 3.25 am. A + B Companies got held up by my own barrage coming from the edge of the wood + put 6 + D 1st in reality	

2353 Wt W2514/1454 700,000 5/15 D. D. & L. A.D.S.S./Forms/C. 2118.

WAR DIARY or INTELLIGENCE SUMMARY

Army Form C. 2118.

Place	Date	Hour	Summary of Events and Information	Remarks and references to Appendices
High Wood	July 20		and in no short time worked right across the wood. At about 1:30am the German shelling the wood heavily and things looking bad to a Shrewsbury reinforcement was asked for. At about 2:45am the R. Welsh Fusiliers came up. Shortly after this the Germans retired from the N.W. corner of the wood and we keep in practically the whole of it. At last the enemy bombarded us heavily with 5.9's. At about midnight the Queen's, K.R.R.C. arrived and relieved the Bn. and took over to Mametz Wood arriving there about 4 A.M. Casualties: killed — Capt. J.E. Burgess ; Lieut. R.B. Ritchie ; 2nd Lieut. McKillop ; 2nd Lieut. Gillespie ; 2nd Lieut. R.H. Laing ; wounded 2nd Lieut. Percy ; 2nd Lieut. McRae ; 2nd Lieut. Rodgers ; 2nd Lt. Bethune ; Major Capt. Evans ; Capt. MacDonald ; 2/Lt. F. Ritchie ; 2nd Lt. Birrey killed 52 ; missing 157 ; wounded 160 ; Roll call	

WAR DIARY
or
INTELLIGENCE SUMMARY.
(Erase heading not required.)

Army Form C. 2118.

Place	Date	Hour	Summary of Events and Information	Remarks and references to Appendices
MAMETZ	Fri 21st	July	Remained at/near MAMETZ and marched at 5 P.M. via outskirts west of BUIRE street and night to [illegible] — Lt. MUNRO	
BUIRE	Sat 22nd		Rested in billets.	
	Sun 23rd		Church parade.	
L'ANCHE	Mon 24th		Marched to north KOTA and H.Q.	
	Tue 25th		8th/4th (129) [illegible] and upkeep. Draft of 46 arrived at dusk & 170 arrived in the afternoon, but no officers.	
	Wed 26th		Training drafts. Lieut gen Chaves, disg., inspected etc.	
	Thu 27th		[illegible] hours inconvenienced by shrapnel [illegible]	
	Fri 28th		Inspection by G.O.C. brigade who expressed himself well pleased	
	Sat 29th		Company parades, training of drafts etc.	
	Sun 30th		Church Parade.	
	Mon 31st		Usual Training.	

[signatures]
Lt Colonel
W.B. The Cameronians

19th Brigade.
33rd Division.

1st BATTALION

SCOTTISH RIFLES (Cameronians)

AUGUST 1916

WAR DIARY
INTELLIGENCE SUMMARY

Army Form C. 2118

1st Manchesters   Vol 25

L.M.
5 sheets

Place	Date	Hour	Summary of Events and Information	Remarks and references to Appendices
BUIRE SUR ANCRE	August 1st		The battalion remained in billets at BUIRE expecting orders to march to the front at any moment. Standing-to continued but every day the enemy's chances of winning now appeared lessening, their lines were being pushed back and training was continued up to the date these were only 10 officers with the 4 companies, only one officer arriving per week having joined.	
	2nd			
	3rd			
	4th			
	5th			
SUR SECOND	6th		The Bn. marched with the Brigade to a point between RECORDEL & MÉAULTE where it went into bivouac as Reserve Brigade to the 106th Brigade being in front line and 98th in support.	
	7th		Remained in bivouac, large fatigue parties supplied for road making. Remainder continued training.	
	8th			
	9th		Training continued & Lewis Gunner, signallers and trench 2d Bns. arms awarded to M.G., Guns for joint work in recent operations.	
	10th			
	11th		Large fatigues on batteries roads during the period.	

Army Form C. 2118.

WAR DIARY
or
INTELLIGENCE SUMMARY
(Erase heading not required.)

Instructions regarding War Diaries and Intelligence Summaries are contained in F.S. Regs., Part II. and the Staff Manual respectively. Title Pages will be prepared in manuscript.

Place	Date	Hour	Summary of Events and Information	Remarks and references to Appendices
Near BECORDEL	Aug 12th		Training etc. continued as before.	
	13th Sun		The brigade moved up into support in the entry line of the morning. 1 Battn. to MAMETZ WOOD, 2 Battn. to FRICOURT, to Cameronians remaining in bivouac as before.	
	14th		Long fatigue parties.	
	15th		5 Second Lieuts. arrived from the 2nd Battn.	
	16th		Long fatigue parties. 5 second lieuts arrived from the 10th Battn.	
	17th		Battn. ordered to be in instant readiness to move after 2 P.M. in connection with an attack on German lines, at 2:45 P.M.	
	18th		Fell in at 7.30 P.M. and marched to MAMETZ WOOD. Only 20 officers went up with the Battn. remainder being left with the transport near FRICOURT.	
			Casualties	
			Killed 4 O.R. Wounded 4 O.R.	

2449 Wt. W14957/M90 750,000 1/16 J.B.C. & A. Forms/C.2118/12.

Army Form C. 2118.

WAR DIARY
or
INTELLIGENCE SUMMARY
(Erase heading not required.)

Place	Date 1916	Hour	Summary of Events and Information	Remarks and references to Appendices
near HIGH WOOD	Aug 19th	12.30 AM	The Battn. moved up to relieve the 4th King's (98th Brigade) who were believed to have taken part of WOOD LANE from the Germans.	
		5 AM	The relief was completed by 5 AM. It was found on arrival that the 4th King's were much depleted, and that their night attack of 98th Brigade appeared to have been fiercely failed, but their position on the night of left, on arrival to have been held by the 2nd R.W.F. and 5th Scottish Rifles. Post on the his own R & L. respectively.	
BAZENTIN LE GRAND		2 PM	At 2 PM the Battn. was withdrawn to near BAZENTIN LE GRAND, its being taken over by the 5th Scottish Rifles. Casualties killed — 1 O.R. wounded — 17 O.R. Reinforcements Suffolk — 1 O.R. Lieut 1 O.R. wounded — 7 O.R. Remained in Suffolk Casualties wounded — 18 O.R.	
	Sun 20			
	21			

WAR DIARY or INTELLIGENCE SUMMARY

Army Form C. 2118.

Place	Date	Hour	Summary of Events and Information	Remarks and references to Appendices
HIGH WOOD	Aug 22		At 6 A.M. the Hte. began to move up to HIGH WOOD by companies taking over trenches held from the 2nd R. Welch Fusiliers. The 20th Roy. L. Fus. relieved us the line on our Right. Casualties - killed 1 O.R. wounded 7 O.R.	
"	23rd		Heavy shelling of the front trenches all morn. & comparatively quiet day. Casualties - wounded 2/Lt J.M. MILLER killed - 1 O.R. 7 O.R.	
"	24th		An attack was made all along the line at 6 P.M., the Bttn. however remained holding the trench in HIGH WOOD. The 100th Brigade on our right took some trenches. Casualties wounded - 11 O.R. killed - 2/Lt J.H. MacVae	
"	25th		Remained in HIGH WOOD.	

WAR DIARY or INTELLIGENCE SUMMARY

(Erase heading not required.)

Army Form C. 2118

Place	Date	Hour	Summary of Events and Information	Remarks and references to Appendices
BAZENTIN le Petit	August 26th		Front held by E. Bay & E. Surrey at crossroads and heavy rainstorm during the day.	
—	Sept 27th		On the evening unit took to POMMIER Redoubt in support to 98th Regt. A miserable place in shelter for Officers & men.	
POMMIER Redoubt	28th		Fatigue party to front line at night.	
FRICOURT WOOD	29th		Moved to FRICOURT WOOD at 7 a.m. Area which still full of & trench occupied by the 5th hm Platoon. Casualties 1 killed, 2 wounded.	
—	30th		Rain all day, everyone wet. Men not employed.	
—	31st		At 8 a.m. the Bn. paraded & marched to RIBEMONT to division being relieved by the 24th Divn.	

J.C. Stewart Maj. for Lieut Colonel
Comdg. 1/13.. the Cameronians

SECRET.

D.A.G. (Theo; H.Q. 19th Inf'y Bde,
General Head Quarters.
3rd Echelon.
Base.
....

       The War Diary of the battalion under my command for the month of September 1916 is forwarded herewith.

30th September 1916. /HCHSmith/ Major,
Commanding, 1st Bn: The Cameronians.

Army Form C. 2118.

WAR DIARY
INTELLIGENCE SUMMARY
(Erase heading not required.)

1st Mannemanian September 1916

Instructions regarding War Diaries and Intelligence Summaries are contained in F. S. Regs., Part II. and the Staff Manual respectively. Title Pages will be prepared in manuscript.

Place	Date 1916	Hour	Summary of Events and Information	Remarks and references to Appendices
MILLENCOURT and BOIS	1st Sept		Bn. marched at 9.30 am from RIBEMONT. Halted for an hour for dinner on route, arrived at M-n-B at 3 p.m. Parties were employed in camp.	
VACQUERIE	2nd		(about 10 miles) Left M-n-B at 8 am, marched via FIENVILLERS to VACQUERIE at 5.30 p.m. (about 16 miles) there were no facilities for hiring transport, & had to make many halts for ½ hour.	
BONLEMONT & BEAUF	3rd 4th		Bn. was carried in lorries & halted in billets.	
VILLERS L'HÔPITAL	4th 5th		Marched to V-l'H. about 9 miles	
ŒUF	5th		Marched to ŒUF about 10 miles	
CROISETTE	6th		Marched to C. about 3 miles	
"	7th		Remained in CROISETTE. The division transferred from XVIIth Corps to VIIth Corps. (General Snow.)	

2449 Wt. W14957/M90 750,000 1/16 J.B.C. & A. Forms/C.2118/12.

Army Form C. 2118.

WAR DIARY
INTELLIGENCE SUMMARY

(Erase heading not required.)

Place	Date	Hour	Summary of Events and Information	Remarks and references to Appendices
	1916 September			
CROISETTE	7th		Divl. attn changed from VIMY to debut of GOMMECOURT	
SERICOURT	8th		Marched to SERICOURT about 6 miles.	
LE SOUICH	9th		Marched to LE SOUICH about 9 miles.	
BIENVILLERS au BOIS	10th		Marched at 8 AM, dinners en route, got to BIENVILLERS 4 PM (about 15 miles). 3 Coys billeted in BIGNV^ES remainder to dugouts on to FONQUEVILLERS. Relieved in Batt. of 51st Bgde. 17th Divn	
BIENVILLERS au BOIS	11th	8.9PM	Relieved 7th Bn Lincolnshire Regt 51st Bde in Z sector (Right B^n) FONQUE- VILLERS. The night was very quiet except for a certain amount of machine gun fire.	
FONQUEVILLERS	12th		The day was quiet with the exception of some shell fire on the support line Wombats. 3 men were slightly wounded. Our artillery were active from 10.30 PM - 11.30 PM. The enemy retaliated with Lt 2 guns but not here Abt 20 shells were sent over —	N° 43022 P^te Nobles N° 22131 P^te Kavanagh N° 17453 P^te Carter N° 4067 P^te King

WAR DIARY
or
INTELLIGENCE SUMMARY

(Erase heading not required.)

Army Form C. 2118.

Place	Date	Hour	Summary of Events and Information	Remarks and references to Appendices
Z Sector FONQUEVILLERS	Sept 13th		The day was again quiet on the whole but the enemy sent over a few light mortars from the direction of "Little Z". During the night there were intermittent machine gun fire by ourselves & also by the enemy.	
"	14th		Hostile trench mortar action during the morning and again in the late afternoon. The top of ROBERTS AVENUE knocked in but otherwise little damage done.	
"	15th		Reinforcement from the 2/9th Royal Scots of 123 NCO's & men — Some machine gun fire and shelling at Stand to in the morning one man was seriously wounded. Since died of wounds. Reinforcement from the 2/9th R. Scots of 110 NCO's & men. Relieved by 6th London Rifles. Marched back to billets in POMMIER.	DW Nº 4/52/13 Pte Murphy

WAR DIARY

INTELLIGENCE SUMMARY

Army Form C. 2118.

Place	Date	Hour	Summary of Events and Information	Remarks and references to Appendices
POMMIER	Sept 16		All men cleaning up in the morning.	
		1 PM	Working party of 160 men for R.E. in trenches. 20 men for Town Major.	
		6 PM	Working parties of 40 men for R.E. in trenches.	
	17th		A few men were able to have baths. As men had been on fatigue all the night before there was no Church parade.	
	18th		The weather made it impossible to do any Parades, visits Kit etc of drafts inspected.	
		1 PM	Work parties. 300 men for R.E. in trenches. Also 20 men for Town Major.	
	19th	9 AM	Work parties. 300 men for R.E. in Trenches. 20 men for Town Major. Remainder of men paraded with their Companies and in arrangements. Pontoro and horse swimming paraded in afternoon under Boutry & Co officers. 2/Lts under Sgt Major. One company has baths.	

WAR DIARY or INTELLIGENCE SUMMARY

Army Form C. 2118.

Place	Date	Hour	Summary of Events and Information	Remarks and references to Appendices
POMMIER	Sept 20th	9 AM	200 men to working parties with R.E. in Fonchevillers 20 men for Town Mayor	
		8 PM	Relieved 6 Scottish Rifles in "Z" Right Sector. Night very quiet.	
FONQUE-VILLERS	21st		Quiet generally but hostile artillery fired about a dozen 4.2 & heavies into the front line at the junction of front line with CORK ST. The trenches dried up with during the afternoon & a good deal of work was able to be done on the cleaning of the trenches in consequence. During the night there was exceptionally little machine gun fire. In other respects night was quiet.	Killed 7/764 l/Cpl Taylor 22544 Pte Turnhouse Wounded 2/Lieut Pepper 2/Lt Craft N° A762 Pte Todd 1156 Cpl Sutcliffe 24517 Pte Payton 14359 Pte Pinnick
	22nd		During the morning enemy again shelled CORK ST. with 4.2's. He also spotted a working party in the BARRICADE & shelled them with 77 m.m. in consequence. 18th un 3 men wounded. 3 men killed. Trenches much drier.	
	23rd		Enemy very quiet. Occasional machine gun fire. One man wounded.	

WAR DIARY
INTELLIGENCE SUMMARY

(Erase heading not required.)

Army Form C. 2118.

Place	Date	Hour	Summary of Events and Information	Remarks and references to Appendices
FONQUEVILLERS	Sept 24th		by M.G. fire. Whilst on Sentry. A few light mortar bombs put into CALVAIRE KEEP. Quiet during the morning. In the afternoon enemy shelled SNIPERS SQUARE with 4.2s and later west of FONQUEVILLERS. In the evening enemy fired some aerial torpedoes. His machine guns were active harassing the front line with Machine gun fire.	Authority No. 112/65 R.E. Sullivan
	25th		The morning quiet except for a few 77 m.m shells. Our heavy artillery very active during morning. Trenches quite dry again. Receipt in one or two places. Early in the night enemy fired some heavy mortars into CALVAIRE KEEP. Our 18 pr retaliates, which had the effect of keeping him quiet for the rest of the night. 40 men were sent to BIENVILLERS every alternate hour for batts throughout the day.	
	26th		Enemy quiet all day, except for about five 4.2 shells which fell in the vicinity of our front line at CORK ST. Battn. carrying all's any. 5th Sufford Rifles. Relief complete without incident. Relieved by 5th Sufford Rifles. Battn in ST AMAND.	
		7:31 AM	The Battn marched back to billets in ST AMAND. Nothing further. for R.E. at 9.45 PM D 3.45 AM of 1 officer & 50 O.R.	

Army Form C. 2118.

WAR DIARY
or
INTELLIGENCE SUMMARY
(Erase heading not required.)

Instructions regarding War Diaries and Intelligence summaries are contained in F. S. Regs., Part II. and the Staff Manual respectively. Title Pages will be prepared in manuscript.

Place	Date	Hour	Summary of Events and Information	Remarks and references to Appendices
ST AMAND	Sept 27th		Companies cleaned up. A few men not previously sent to baths, were marched to GAUDIEMPRÉ.	
"	28th		PARADES. Recruit drafts paraded under R.S.M. for drill — Remainder of Companies paraded for Physical Training — Bayonet fighting & class not drill — Lewis Gunners & Bombers paraded under their own specialist officers. Reinforcement of 18 O.R. from 4th Seaforth Rifles. 17 Lewis Gunners Readers.	
"	29th		Wet all morning. Officers lectures to their companies. In the afternoon the N.C.O's paraded under the Regimental Sergeant Major.	
LUCHEUX	30th		The Battalion paraded at 8 A.M. & marched to LUCHEUX (about 10 miles).	31/9/16

/C. Hh.../L. hugh
Comdg. 4th The Cameronians

SECRET

D.A.G.
    General Head Quarters.
        3rd Echelon.
           Base.
....

    Herewith War Diary for the month of October 1916.

2nd November 1916.

                              Major
              Commanding, 1st Bn: The Cameronians.

WAR DIARY or INTELLIGENCE SUMMARY

Army Form C. 2118

Place	Date	Hour	Summary of Events and Information	Remarks and references to Appendices
LUCHEUX	Oct 1st		Parades in morning till 10 A.M. Church Parade 10.30 A.M. G.O.C Division attended. Afterwards he lectured Officers & N.C.O's. In afternoon inspection of Clothing, both Bns.	
	2nd	9-12	Drill Parade. Two Officers attended tactical exercise (in trout Lotch(?)) held by the Division.	
		2.30	Rain all afternoon made it impossible to do any parade.	
	3rd		Rain in the early part of the morning, cleared later. Parade under company arrangements carried out.	
	4th		Rain during morning. Parade a little about 11 o'clock. Conference were use to trade.	
	5th		The battalion paraded at 9 A.M. to practise in attacking formations and extensions. I attended as a [illegible] to [illegible] of the men, whom Br. O'Brien of the Brigade.	

WAR DIARY or INTELLIGENCE SUMMARY

Army Form C. 2118.

(Erase heading not required.)

Place	Date	Hour	Summary of Events and Information	Remarks and references to Appendices
LUCHEUX	Oct 6th		4 Officers left by motor bus at 7 p.m. to visit trenches in front of HEBUTERNE from which the Bn. is to attack in a few days time.	
"	7th		4 more Officers visited the trenches. Training by companies.	
"	8th Sun		Bn. paraded at 8 A.M. and marched to DOULLENS where the Brigade practised the attack. The German trenches being marked out on the ground. A very wet day.	
"	9th		In the afternoon Officers attended a tactical exercise in DOULLENS. Bn. to practice formations to be used in the attack in conjunction with 5th S.R. Carried out a practice attack on a wood (near OPPY)	
"	10th		The Battn. moved in 40 buses to SOUASTRE & thence by route march to SAILLY-AU-BOIS and HEBUTERNE arriving at 7 P.M. Took over front line with 1 Coy relieving 1 Coy of 7th LINCOLNS.	
"	11th	2 P.M.	1 Coy Staged in HEBUTERNE 2 in SAILLY.	

WAR DIARY or INTELLIGENCE SUMMARY

Army Form C. 2118.

Places	Date 1916	Hour	Summary of Events and Information	Remarks and references to Appendices
HEBUTERNE	11 (Oct)		Casualties:— Pte. Portfield, Dunkley, Green (B Coy), wounded	
"	12		Artillery cutting enemy wire, patrols out by night to inspect. Enemy reply slight.	
"	13		Casualties:— Pte Cleaver, L/c Ramm, Pte Robertson — wounded. Wire cutting continued, wire not being noticeable. Enemy shelling increased. C & D Coys relieved A & B at dusk.	
"	14		Casualties:— Pte McCabe, wounded.	
"	15		Found Lieut. — 3 Officers joined from 2/5 Scottish Rifles. 2 Coys. up were relieved in afternoon by the 5th S.R. and the whole Battn. moved back to bivouac in BAYEN COURT. Sgt. Bottomache, No 43208 Pte Wilson killed. 3 O.R. wounded Casualties in trenches.	
BAYENCOURT	16		Remained in bivouac, large fatigue parties to the front line.	
"	17		Bn. paraded at 4 P.M. and marched to SOUASTRE. (3 m.) Then in busses to IVERNY arriving at 8 P.M.	
IVERNY	18		Orders received at 3 a.m. to march again. Paraded at 7 a.m. + marched to DOULLENS arriving it 10.30 AM.	
DOULLENS				

Army Form C. 2118.

WAR DIARY
or
INTELLIGENCE SUMMARY
(Erase heading not required.)

Instructions regarding War Diaries and Intelligence Summaries are contained in F. S. Regs., Part II. and the Staff Manual respectively. Title Pages will be prepared in manuscript.

Place	Date	Hour	Summary of Events and Information	Remarks and references to Appendices
DOULLENS	Oct 19th 1916	19/16	Paraded at 12.30 p.m. and marched 2 miles out. After went by l.h.mes train arrived. Proceeded to BUIRE-SUR-ANCRE via AMIENS arriving about 9. P.M. Transport still unived (Lord Crewen) proceeded by road. Billets in XIV Corps. Billets in BUIRE-CORBIE SUR ANCRE	
VILLE sous BUIRE-HEUR CORBIE	20th		Remained in Billets at VILLE-SUR-ANCRE	
ANCRE	21st		Paraded 8 AM and marched to The CITADEL (about 5 miles) drew country - Going very bad 2 or 3½ not arriving at our destination til 1.30 PM	
	22nd		Paraded 10.20 AM and marched to BRIQUETERIE nr BERNAFAY WOOD - about 5 miles across country, arrived 2.30 PM Battalion in trenches. Reinforcement of 9 officers from 1/5 Scottish Rifles + other details.	
	23rd		Paraded 7 A.M. & marched to GUILLEMONT. The 19th Bn in Reserve 6th & DIV's which attacked at 2.30 PM	

2449 Wt. W14957/M90 750,000 1/16 J.B.C. & A. Forms/C.2118/12.

WAR DIARY
or
INTELLIGENCE SUMMARY
(Erase heading not required.)

Army Form C. 2118.

Place	Date	Hour	Summary of Events and Information	Remarks and references to Appendices
GUILLEMONT	1916 24th		Remained in Reserve at GUILLEMONT. B ECHELON at CARNOY. Work done to improve shelters & camp generally.	
"	25th		Remained in GUILLEMONT	
"	26th		Carrying parties for bomb & trench stores to R.W. Fusiliers	
"	27th		Orders received to relieve R.W. Fusiliers in trenches E of LESBOEUFS. - MORVAL 2/Lt Huxtable & one wounded by shell fire. Passed 4.30 p.m.	
LESBOEUFS	28th		Orders received for the Battalion to attack HAZY TRENCH in conjunction with 5th Scottish Rifles on a 1 company front. Heavy shelling. 6 men killed 14 wounded.	
"	29th		Attack on HAZY TRENCH by D Coy at 5.45 a.m. No preliminary bombardment. Company enfiladed from a gut by M.G. fire & suffered heavy casualties & were unable to gain their objective. To lay out & entrenched themselves 50y in front of BARITSKA TRENCH.	
			CASUALTIES CAPT BRICKMANN killed. 2/Lts Argna, Cameron, Boyd, many	

Army Form C. 2118.

WAR DIARY
or
INTELLIGENCE SUMMARY
(Erase heading not required.)

Instructions regarding War Diaries and Intelligence Summaries are contained in F.S. Regs., Part II. and the Staff Manual respectively. Title Pages will be prepared in manuscript.

Place	Date	Hour	Summary of Events and Information	Remarks and references to Appendices
	29th		2/Lt Dalrymple wounded. Casualties in other ranks 17 killed, 49 wounded, 33 missing.	
	30th		Relieved by 9th R.H.L.I. 96th Bde. Battalion moved back into shelters at BRIQUETERIE near BERNAFAY WOOD	
	31st		Men cleaning up	

R.C. Whom Lt Col.
Commdg the Cameronians

1/8/16

WAR DIARY
INTELLIGENCE SUMMARY

(Erase heading not required.)

Army Form C. 2118.

November 1916
1st Cameronians
Vol 29

2H.M.
4 sheets

Place	Date	Hour	Summary of Events and Information	Remarks and references to Appendices
BRIQUETERIE	1st		Men cleaning up and drying their clothes. Working Party carrying flare boards from GINCHY to FLERS LINE (2 miles)	
	2nd		Working Party 8.15 A.M. Carrying flare boards from TRONES WOOD to FLANK ALLEY	
			Skirting Bearer Party (50 men) to GINCHY Dressing Stn. 19th R.B. relieved 9th Bn. Battalion in Reserve. relieved ARGYLL's	
TRONES WOOD	3rd		SUTHERLAND H's in TRONES WOOD	
TRONES WOOD	4th		Battalion remained in TRONES WOOD	
	5th		Battalion moved at 3 A.M. to the FLERS LINE, forming with 5th Scottish Rifles Reserve to 23rd Div., who were attacking in conjunction with 1st Div's on the left & French on the right.	
FLERS LINE	6th		Cameron working Party. Very Quiet not at all a time for 3 hours steam	

WAR DIARY
or
INTELLIGENCE SUMMARY

(Erase heading not required.)

Instructions regarding War Diaries and Intelligence Summaries are contained in F.S. Regs., Part II. and the Staff Manual respectively. Title Pages will be prepared in manuscript.

Place	Date	Hour	Summary of Events and Information	Remarks and references to Appendices
FLERS LINE	Nov. 1916 7th		Relieved by another Coy of my — Working Parties continued — 1 Company at 2 hours notice to reinforce R W Fusiliers. Relieved by 2/Scottish Rifles of 23rd Bde 8 "D" Battalion marched back to Huts near CARNOY.	
CARNOY	8		Battalion paraded 9.45 AM & marched across country to HÉAULTÉ & billeted there.	
HÉAULTÉ	9		Men cleaning up. Transport left by road for HALLENCOURT area.	
"	10th		Inspection of kits etc.	
"	11th		Batt. paraded at 9 am. marched to BUIRE, where entrained. Train started 12. noon. Arrived AIRAISNES 1 am. marched to CITERNE (6½ miles) arriving there 4·30 a.m.	
CITERNE	12th			

Army Form C. 2118.

WAR DIARY
INTELLIGENCE SUMMARY
(Erase heading not required.)

November 1916

Instructions regarding War Diaries and Intelligence Summaries are contained in F. S. Regs., Part II. and the Staff Manual respectively. Title Pages will be prepared in manuscript.

Place	Date	Hour	Summary of Events and Information	Remarks and references to Appendices
CITERNE	Nov 1916			
	13th		Cleaning up	
	14th		Squad and Company drill	
	15		Company drill	
	16		Brigade route march	
	17		Baths for B and D Companies. Training	
	18		Baths at HALLENCOURT for "A" and "C" Companies	
	19	Sun	Church parades	
	20		Training. Company drill	
	21		Training. "A" Company on the range	
	22		Training. Company drill. Bayonet fighting. "B" Coy on the range	
	23		Inspection by G.O.C. 33rd Division, who expressed himself pleased with the appearance and turn out of the men.	
	24		Brigade route march	
	25		Training. Kit Inspection	
	26	Sun	Church Parades	
	27		Training. Company drill. "C" Coy on the range	

Army Form C. 2118.

WAR DIARY
or
INTELLIGENCE SUMMARY
(Erase heading not required.)

November 1916

Place	Date	Hour	Summary of Events and Information	Remarks and references to Appendices
CITERNE	28 Tues		Training. Company drill. £ "D" Company on the range	
	29		Training. Company drill. £ "A" Company on the range	
	30		Training. Football match against the 2nd Battalion. Their team came over from AUMATRE. Result 5 goals to nil in their favour. The Officers dined at AUMATRE with the Officers of the 2nd Battalion.	

L. Lent Colonel
D. Cruivenen
Cmdg 1/12

2/12/16

Army Form C. 2118.

WAR DIARY
or
INTELLIGENCE SUMMARY
(Erase heading not required.)

No. ...1.../13. The Caernarvon ... December 1916

C.E. 29

Instructions regarding War Diaries and Intelligence Summaries are contained in F.S. Regs., Part II. and the Staff Manual respectively. Title Pages will be prepared in manuscript.

25/11
7 sheets

Place	Date	Hour	Summary of Events and Information	Remarks and references to Appendices
CITERNE	DEC 1st		Baths at HALLENCOURT for 2 Companies — Remaining 2 Companies on Brigade Route March.	
	2nd		Baths for 2 companies — Remaining 2 companies Route March.	
	3rd		Church Parade for all denominations. Preparations made	
	4th		for moving up the line.	
	5th		Parades under company arrangements.	
			Reinforcement of 14 O.R.	
	6th		Parades under Company arrangements.	
			Draft of 49 O.R.	
	7th		Parades under Company arrangements.	
			Transport moved at 7 A.M. in advance of the battalion moving	

2449 Wt. W14957/M90 750,000 1/16 J.B.C. & A. Forms/C.2118/12.

Army Form C. 2118.

WAR DIARY
or
INTELLIGENCE SUMMARY
(Erase heading not required.)

Place	Date	Hour	Summary of Events and Information	Remarks and references to Appendices
CITERNE	DEC 7th		Rest Day—	
	DEC 8		Battalion marched to AIRAINES from CITERNE, starting at 6.40 A.m, and entrained there for MERICOURT from there marched to VAUX-SUR-SOMME, where the battalion bivouaced for the night.	
VAUX-SUR-SOMME	9th		Paraded 1.30 P.M & marched to Camp 111 near BRAY (12 miles) arriving 5.30 P.M. Draft 53 O.R.	
CAMP 111	10th		Day spent in cleaning up.	
"	11th		Paraded 10 A.M. marched across country to CAMP 17 near SUSANNE. Transport by MARICOURT road. Draft 120 O.R.	
CAMP 17	12th		Improvements made in camp & also clearing the surroundings. Shell...	

Army Form C. 2118.

WAR DIARY
or
INTELLIGENCE SUMMARY
(Erase heading not required.)

Instructions regarding War Diaries and Intelligence Summaries are contained in F. S. Regs., Part II. and the Staff Manual respectively. Title Pages will be prepared in manuscript.

Place	Date	Hour	Summary of Events and Information	Remarks and references to Appendices
CAMP 14	DEC 12th		has been left in a very insanitary condition. C.O. 2 Company Commanders reconnoitred road to Trenches. Improvements to Camp continued.	
	13th			
	14th		Battalion paraded 1·30 P.M. to march to Trenches at RANCOURT. 150 men per company inclusive of Lewis Gunners & Battalion HQ Taken. "B" Echelon at MAUREPAS. 3 Officers & 170 O.R. left for trenches remained in CAMP 17. Battalion took over from 16th K.R.R. Trenches very wet & muddy. No work was possible by day by night a certain amount of work was done to improve the line but casualties were chiefly occupied in carrying.	
Trenches	15th			

Army Form C. 2118.

WAR DIARY
or
INTELLIGENCE SUMMARY
(Erase heading not required.)

Place	Date	Hour	Summary of Events and Information	Remarks and references to Appendices
Trenches	Dec 16th		During the night the 2 companies in front line were relieved by the Support & Reserve Companies. 1 man killed, 2 wounded.	
	17th		Day comparatively quiet, except for a little shelling. 4 men wounded.	
	18th		During the day there was rather heavy shelling of the front line. There were only a few Casualties. Five men killed and eleven wounded. The battalion was relieved by 25th R.F. at about 9 P.M. and went back into Support at PRIEZ FARM. One Company was sent up to LE FOREST. Working party of 200 men sent up to front line during the night.	
	19th		Working parties again sent up to front line (trenches)	

WAR DIARY
or
INTELLIGENCE SUMMARY
(Erase heading not required.)

Place	Date	Hour	Summary of Events and Information	Remarks and references to Appendices
Trenches	Dec 21st		Working party (150) for front line, for laying floor boards. One man wounded.	
	22nd		Lt. & Qr. Mr. G. WOOD 1st Bt. The Cameronians was tried by Court Martial, charge with Drunkenness. He was found guilty of the charge and the Court sentenced him to be severely reprimanded. Battalion relieved by 1st/13th Middlesex Regt. & brought down in motor lorries to Camp 17 arriving about 10 P.M.	
Camp 17	23rd		Companies cleaning up. L.O. inspected Companies.	
	24th		G.O.C. inspected the Battalion. Church Parade Service 10.30 A.M.	
	25th		CHRISTMAS DAY.	

WAR DIARY
or
INTELLIGENCE SUMMARY

(Erase heading not required.)

Army Form C. 2118.

Place	Date	Hour	Summary of Events and Information	Remarks and references to Appendices
CAMP 12	Dec 26		Battalion paraded 10:30 A.M. and marched to CAMP via BRAY	
"	27th		Transport left 7 A.M. to march to – Battalion paraded 12 Noon to march to EDGE HILL. Entrained at and PONT-REMY 10 PM arrived in billets at 10:45 6 P.M. Battalion billets in two villages EAUCOURT and P.M. EPAGNE.	
EPAGNE	28th		Companies cleaning up.	
"	29		Kit inspections in the morning – Drill parade from 2 PM – 3 PM.	
"	30th		Companies paraded from 9 – 12:30 N.C.Os under R.S.M. at 2 P.M. Lecture to officers by M.O.	

Army Form C. 2118.

WAR DIARY
or
INTELLIGENCE SUMMARY
(Erase heading not required.)

Place	Date	Hour	Summary of Events and Information	Remarks and references to Appendices
EPAGNE	Dec 31st	10.30 A.M.	Church Parade	

K.C.Smith Major
Comdg. 1/B. 7th Cameron

Army Form C. 2118.

WAR DIARY
INTELLIGENCE SUMMARY
(Erase heading not required.)

Macedonia
Vol 30

26.11
J sheets

Place	Date	Hour	Summary of Events and Information	Remarks and references to Appendices
EPAGNE	1917 Jan 1st		Holiday.	
	2nd	9-10	Each Platoon paraded as strong as possible to carry out new training (ie Fighting Platoon)	
		10.30	Physical Training & Bayonet fighting – Company Drill	
		12.30	8th Company firing on 30 x range Classes for Lewis Gunners under Specialist Officers Range & Lewis Gun under R.S.M.	
		2-3 P.M.	C.O. inspected Companies (as strong as possible) in Field Service marching order. Afterwards Companies paraded under their own arrangement.	
	3rd	2 P.M. 4 P.M.	1 Company on range 1 Company extended Order Drill & Artillery formation. Battn Pastor started running shorts for a day to bath.	

Place	Date	Hour	Summary of Events and Information	Remarks and references to Appendices
EPAGNE	1917 Jan 3rd	5.30 P.M.	2 Companies light operations —	
	"4th	9 AM	Platoon Parades as before in possible -	
		10.30	Companies carried out physical training & Bayonet fighting)	
		-12.30	Company Drill	
	"5th	9.30	Lewis Gun & Bombing Classes under specialist officers — Starting point EAUCOURT Battalion route march — BRAY - EPAGNE X roads. Route BELLIFONTAIN - BRAY - EPAGNE	
		2 PM	1 Company on camp 1 company between mess dinch & Artillery Formation	
		5.20	2 Companies night operations Reinforcement of 8.8 O.R. joined the Battalion -	
	6th	9-10	Platoon Parades as strong as possible	

Army Form C. 2118.

WAR DIARY
or
INTELLIGENCE SUMMARY

(Erase heading not required.)

Instructions regarding War Diaries and Intelligence Summaries are contained in F. S. Regs., Part II. and the Staff Manual respectively. Title Pages will be prepared in manuscript.

Place	Date	Hour	Summary of Events and Information	Remarks and references to Appendices
EPAGNE	Jan 6th	10.30 –12.30	1 Company Range. Remaining Companies Bayonet Fighting, Physical Drill.	
			2nd Company Drill – Lewis Gun & Bombing Classes	
	7th		Church Parade	
			1 Company Ball – (Brigade Baths)	
	8th	9 – 10	Platoon Parades –	
		10.30 –12.30	Companies Drill – Physical Training & Bayonet Fighting. Lewis Gun & Bombing Classes	
		2.15 – 4.15	2 Companies Range. 1 Company Reconnaissance in front of Infantry Commanders. 1 Company Baths	

Army Form C. 2118.

WAR DIARY
or
INTELLIGENCE SUMMARY
(Erase heading not required.)

Instructions regarding War Diaries and Intelligence Summaries are contained in F. S. Regs., Part II. and the Staff Manual respectively. Title Pages will be prepared in manuscript.

Place	Date 1916	Hour	Summary of Events and Information	Remarks and references to Appendices
EPAGNE	Jany 9		Company Training, drill, bayonet fighting etc.	
	10		Lt. Col. Chaplin resumed command of the Battn. Training as usual.	
	11		Brigade route march in direction of BEUVIN COURT. 2 days night operations.	
	12		Company Training. 2 days night operations.	
	13		Battn. paraded for presentation of medal ribbon by the Divil Commander Major General Pinney C.B. The ul/mentioned were decorated. Capt. Brown Milty Cross Reg. Quny Mily medal 2Lt Scott (Offs) " " Pte Anderson " " — Sussex " " Pte Garvey " "	
	14 Sun		Church Parades.	
	15.		The transport left at 7.30 AM on march to its forward area.	

Army Form C. 2118.

WAR DIARY
or
INTELLIGENCE SUMMARY
(Erase heading not required.)

Instructions regarding War Diaries and Intelligence Summaries are contained in F.S. Regs., Part II. and the Staff Manual respectively. Title Pages will be prepared in manuscript.

Place	Date 1917	Hour	Summary of Events and Information	Remarks and references to Appendices
EPAGNE	Jany 16		Training as usual, morning only. Afternoon packing up. Very cold.	
"	17		Battn. paraded at 6 A.M. & marched to PONT REMY (3 miles) to entrain. Train arrived at 11 A.M. Snowing hard & bitterly cold. Detrained at BRAY at 6 p.m. marched to Camp 112. (2 miles)	
Camp 112	18		Remained in Camp 112. Snow on ground about 1 foot.	
"	19		Paraded at 1 P.M. and marched to Camp 18 near SUZANNE. (7 miles) Got in it 4 P.M. Very cold.	
Camp 18	20		Remained in Camp #18. A draft of 81 men joined.	Wounded L/Cpl R. Dunn 165792
Line	21		The Battn. relieved the 2nd Bt 6th Regiment of French 17th Division in the front line in front of CLERY. 3 Coys to N. of SOMME. French 75th corps on right & French 48th Bde (British) left of SOMME. 2 Platoons of C Coy under Capt. E. HUNTER S. of the SOMME. The Battn. is Thus To Right of The British line. Guides met Coys. at CURLU. Total distance to front line about 8 miles.	
Line	22		Transport & C Coy. moved to FRISE bend. In preparing to relieve. Still very cold.	

Army Form C. 2118.

WAR DIARY
or
INTELLIGENCE SUMMARY
(Erase heading not required.)

Instructions regarding War Diaries and Intelligence Summaries are contained in F. S. Regs., Part II. and the Staff Manual respectively. Title Pages will be prepared in manuscript.

Place	Date	Hour	Summary of Events and Information	Remarks and references to Appendices
LINE	23		Enemy fairly quiet. Had front	W.wounded 3/1st Fusiliers
	24		Front still continued. Battn. relieved by 20th R. Fusiliers, went into support at HOWITZER WOOD.	11067 Pte Fergusson 41011 Pte Thomas 40394 Pte Lee Poidovin
HOWITZER WOOD	25		Battalion remained in Howitzer Wood. Inspection of Major H. C. H. Smith to 19th Infy Bde for duty.	
	26		2 Platoons took over south of SOMME from 20th Fusiliers	
			Had front.	
FRISE BEND	27		2 Companies took to FRISE BEND. 1 Company's Support Platoon remained at Howitzer Wood. Coys with the 5th	
LINE	28		continued. Battalion went up into line previous at 4.30 P.M. taking ½ over from 20th Fusiliers. Working party of draft sent up to assist Trench Mortar Btys. He they casualties 1 killed 2 wounded.	14158 Pte Lever 14148 Pte Millen 4739 Pte Sloan 44448 Pte Pinnive
	29th		Quiet day.	
	30th		Enemy quiet except for rifle grenades.	Pte Pinnive

Place	Date	Hour	Summary of Events and Information	Remarks and references to Appendices
SUZANNE	Jan 27 3rd		Battalion relieved by Argyle & Sutherland Highlanders. There were 4 casualties in B Coy coming out. The battalion was brought back in motor buses to SUZANNE.	W. Ewbru 9/39 Sgt Hinks 240506 Pte Payne 40446 P/C Brooker 40414 P/C Black 45630 Pte Park

J. Noll Files
Maj M.R.F. MacCameron

Secret

A.A.G.
 General Head Quarters
  Base.

The War Diary of the battalion under my Command for the month of February 1917 is forwarded herewith.

R.L. Hunter
 Captain
In the Field
1/3/1917   Comdg. 1/Bn The Cameronians

Army Form C. 2118.

WAR DIARY
or
INTELLIGENCE SUMMARY

(Erase heading not required.)

Secret

1/B 7th Canadian
Vol 31

27.11
6 sheets

Place	Date	Hour	Summary of Events and Information	Remarks and references to Appendices
SUZANNE	1917 Feb 1st		Cleaning up after coming out of the trenches — kit inspections.	
	— 2nd		Instruction in use of Small Box Respirator by Divl Gas Offr to Officers & N.C.O.'s in morning — men instructed in afternoon.	
	— 3rd	9 AM	Runners	
		10 AM	Drill. Practice in use of Small Box Respirator	
	— 4th		Church Parade. All men who has been in trenches to bathe.	
	— 4th-5		"Companies" practised the attack.	
	— 6th		Attack practised.	
	— 7th		C.O. & Company Commanders went up to inspect place to be taken over by battalion.	
	— 8th		Battalion Parade 5 pm. marches up to R. A. D. Wood & took over from Norwich Regt 100th Bde in left sector.	
SUPPORT LINE	— 7th		Quiet day except for a little shelling — Three men wounded.	
	— 9th		Permanent working parties putting 3 100 men from batn in HARRIERES WOOD from 9 AM – 5 PM	
	— 10th		Battalion found working parties.	

WAR DIARY
or
INTELLIGENCE SUMMARY
(Erase heading not required.)

Army Form C.2118

Place	Date	Hour	Summary of Events and Information	Remarks and references to Appendices
SUPPORT LINE	Feb 11th		Working parties.	
LINE	12th		Battalion took over from 2nd Royal Fusiliers in the line. Heavy enemy shelling when the battalion was taking over the line but there were no casualties.	
	13th		Enemy artillery active from 5.45 A.M. to about 8 h. Directed against our front & support lines but without much effect. Enemy's rifle active. He also fires some rifle grenades & aerial torpedoes without effect.	
	14th		Our patrols active at night examining enemy wire to find out whether it was sufficiently cut. Enemy quiet. Enemy aeroplane brought down behind his lines opposite sector held by the battalion. Our artillery continues nu cutting. Enemy quiet except for rifle grenades & aerial torpedoes. 2/Lt Walker was wounded.	
	15th			
	16th		The battalion was relieved by 3 coys 10th Royal Fusiliers and 1 coy R.M. Fusiliers. After relief marched back to Hinges.	

Army Form C. 2118.

WAR DIARY
or
INTELLIGENCE SUMMARY
(Erase heading not required.)

Instructions regarding War Diaries and Intelligence Summaries are contained in F. S. Regs., Part II. and the Staff Manual respectively. Title Pages will be prepared in manuscript.

Place	Date	Hour	Summary of Events and Information	Remarks and references to Appendices
HOWITZER WOOD	Feb 15th		WOOD. There were some Casualties before leaving out. There were Killed and 2 wounded from enemys artillery.	
			HOWITZER WOOD	
		6 p.m.	Relief of 2nd R. W. Fusiliers in the QUARRY SECTOR. The battalion also took over from a company frontage of the 11th R.E. Three companies in front line and one in support here Bn. stretcher Headquarters. The left company in very bad trench, partly the wall of the trench in places trench was not more than waist deep.	
		19 p.m.	The enemy was quiet. Not much work was possible except in the night. Our artillery action entirely wire.	

2449 Wt. W14957/M90 750,000 1/16 J.B.C. & A. Forms/C.2118/12.

WAR DIARY
INTELLIGENCE SUMMARY

(Erase heading not required.)

Army Form C. 2118.

Place	Date	Hour	Summary of Events and Information	Remarks and references to Appendices
Trenches	Feb 20		Enemy batching quiet. Except for a few shells on the right company front. Enemy trench mortar active all day.	
	21st		Quiet in both batching or trench mortar. Indn. company relief. The company in support relieving the Left company. This took from 6 noon to complete owing to the heavy state of the ground.	
	22nd		Another quiet day - very little shelling - Trench mortars were active at times during the day.	
	23rd		Enemy bombarded our front line trenches heavily during the evening from 6 P.m onwards.	

R. A. Hunter Capt.
Comdg 1st Cy The Camerons

Army Form C. 2118.

WAR DIARY
or
INTELLIGENCE SUMMARY
(Erase heading not required.)

Place	Date	Hour	Summary of Events and Information	Remarks and references to Appendices
ROAD WOOD	Feb 24th		Battalion relieved by 1st Bn Middlesex. 4th Bn The King's 98th Bde and went back into support in ROAD WOOD.	
	25th		Battalion relieved by 1st Bn. The MIDDLESEX. Owing to one of the guides losing his way the last company were not relieved until 2.45 A.m. Battalion marches back to huts in Camp 19	
	26th			
	27th		Commanders Cleaning up. Battn. to whole Battalion. Inspections.	
	28th		All available men on Road Fatigue. 200 men in morning & afternoon. 50 men to CURLU & to to Camp Commandant.	

WAR DIARY or INTELLIGENCE SUMMARY

(Erase heading not required.)

Army Form C.2118

The Cameronians (Scottish Rifles) Vol 32

March 1917

28.11
7 sheets

Place	Date	Hour	Summary of Events and Information	References to Appendices
CAMP 19	March 1st	9.30 12.30 2-4	Physical Training – Bayonet fighting – Drill Training of Lewis Gunners and Bombers under company arrangements Lewis Gunners & Bombers to training under company specialist officers Remainder of officers & NCO's help ready	
	2nd		Working parties 200 men in morning & afternoon on repairing roads near Vaux. Inspection of rifles & Lewis guns by Armourer Sgt.	
	3rd		Working parties 200 men from A & B Coys. work from 9 A.h. – 4 P.h. C & D Coys Physical Drill, Bayonet Fighting & Drill. Bombers practised throwing bombs with live Grenades. Lewis Gunners on range	
	4th		Church parade in morning. C & D Coys found working parties of 200 men for roads. In afternoon A & B Coys training. Lewis Guns fired on range.	

2449 Wt. W14957/M90 750,000 1/16 J.B.C. & A. Forms/C.2118/12.

WAR DIARY or INTELLIGENCE SUMMARY

Army Form C. 2118.

Place	Date	Hour	Summary of Events and Information	Remarks and references to Appendices
CAMP 19	5th		Battalion paraded at 3.30 P.M. marched up to relieve 1st Queens in the Support line CLERY SECTOR. 2½ Coys in MAUD AVENUE. 2 Platoons in CLERY CHATEAU. 1 Coy 2nd line. B Battalion FRISE BEND	
	6th		There was considerable shelling by enemy & also by our own. A Coy went up to relieve a Coy of R. Fusiliers in support to left Battalion. 2 Platoons near Bn HQ. (I.C. MADALAINE) 2 Platoons MERLIN TRENCH. R Coy relieved by a company of 5th S.R. in 2nd line & moved up to MAUD AVENUE.	
	7th		Quiet all day. The Battalion relieved by 17th Welch Regt 40th Divt. marches took to billets in SUZANNE. Arrived 11.30 P.M.	
	8th		Battalion paraded 9 A.M. & marches by BRAY to CAMP 13 about 6 miles journey back.	

WAR DIARY or INTELLIGENCE SUMMARY

Army Form C. 2118.

(Erase heading not required.)

Instructions regarding War Diaries and Intelligence Summaries are contained in F. S. Regs., Part II. and the Staff Manual respectively. Title Pages will be prepared in manuscript.

Place	Date	Hour	Summary of Events and Information	Remarks and references to Appendices
CAMBS	9th		Cleaning up Intytrelam.	
	10th	9-10	Platoon Training (in thing in front of)	
		10-12	Special it under their own offices	
			Company Drill – Physical training – Bayonet Fighting.	
		2-4	Lectures were Drill – Artillery Formation	
	11th		Church Parade	
	12th	7.30	Running	
		12	Inspection by G.O.C. 33rd Division (Gen Pinney)	
	13th	7.30	Running	
			Battn. for whole Battalion	
			Instruction to 2 Companies by Capt. Bayonet Instructor	
	14th	7.30	Bayonet Squading – Bayonet Fighting – Route Marching	
		10-12	Platoon Training	
		2-4	(further training)	

Army Form C. 2118.

WAR DIARY
or
INTELLIGENCE SUMMARY

(Erase heading not required.)

Instructions regarding War Diaries and Intelligence Summaries are contained in F. S. Regs., Part II. and the Staff Manual respectively. Title Pages will be prepared in manuscript.

Place	Date	Hour	Summary of Events and Information	Remarks and references to Appendices
CAMP 13	May 15th	9 AM	Company Route march CHIPILLY - SAILLY-LAURETTE - BRAY CORBIE Road - CAMP 13. Artillery formation from column of route practised.	
		2 PM	Platoon Training	
		3 PM	Regtl Lectures for Officers on 3 Platoon Sections - Outpost scheme	
	16th	7.30	Running	
		9-10	Bayonet Fighting - Bombing - Rifle loading	
		10-12	2 Coy Platoon Training - 2 coy Trench D. 99 my	
		2 PM	Platoon Training	
		6 -	Brigade Lecture	
	17th	9-10	Bayonet Fighting - Bombing - Rifle loading	
		10-12	Platoon Training	
		12.10 AM	Church Parade	

WAR DIARY
or
INTELLIGENCE SUMMARY

(Erase heading not required.)

Army Form C. 2118.

Place	Date	Hour	Summary of Events and Information	Remarks and references to Appendices
CAMP 13	May 19	7.40	Reveille	
		9-10	Training under Section Commanders	
		10-10.30	Drill	
		10.30-1pm	Reconnaissance in the direction of ETINEHAM	
		2 pm	Specialist Training	
			Brigade instructors trotting in Welding formation	
	2nd	9 am	Company route march. Camp 13 – CHIPILLY – ETINEHAM – BRAY CORBIE	
			road	
		2 pm	Specialist Training	
		3 pm	Regtl. Scheme. Putting CHIPILLY in state of defence	
		7.40	Reveille	
		9 am	Training under Section Commanders	
		10-1	2 Coy ATTACK & DEFENCE. 2 Coy ADVANCE & REAR Guard	
		2pm	Specialist Training	

Army Form C. 2118.

WAR DIARY
or
INTELLIGENCE SUMMARY

(Erase heading not required.)

Instructions regarding War Diaries and Intelligence Summaries are contained in F. S. Regs., Part II. and the Staff Manual respectively. Title Pages will be prepared in manuscript.

Place	Date	Hour	Summary of Events and Information	Remarks and references to Appendices
CAMP 11	March 22	7.30	Reveille	
		9 am	Training under Section Commanders	
		10	Practice in the Box Respirator	
		10.30	Company in attack from Artillery formation	
		2	Stand at Training	
	23rd	9 am	Company Route March CAMP 11 - MORLANCOURT - SAILLY LAURETTE	
			Artillery formation practice when returning train for lunch	
		2	Stand at Training	
		3	Regtl Exercise. Attack on a position	
	24th	7.10	Reveille	
		9	Training under Section Commanders	
		10-1	2 hrs Attack & Defence. 2 hrs Advance to Rear Guard	
	25th	11 am	Church Parade. G.O.C. attended. Afterwards parade moved to Ethnets	
	26th		Wet all day. Training carried out in huts.	
	27th	9 am to 9 am	Brigade Route March. CHIPILLY - CERISY - SAILLY LAURETTE - BRAY CORBIE 2nd - CAMP 13. Brigade Conference	

WAR DIARY or INTELLIGENCE SUMMARY

Army Form C. 2118.

Place	Date	Hour	Summary of Events and Information	Remarks and references to Appendices
CAMP 13	March 28th	9 A.M.	Section Training	
		10 a.m.	All Companies had lecture.	
		2 P.M.	Gas demonstration.	
	29th	9 A.M.	Section Training	
		10-12:30	2 Companies Advanced to Rifle grenade. 1 Company Platoon Training. 1 Company Lecture Digging (String Point)	
			Remainder of the day was wet and there was no training for other Companies.	
	30		Specialist training in huts.	
		9.30	Route March. Camp 13 — CHIPILLY CEMETRY — MERICOURT — MORCOURT	
		2	CHIPILLY - CAMP 13 - Specialist training	
	31st	9 A.M.	Section Training	
		10-12:30	2 Companies Intensive Digging. 1 Company Wiring. 1 Co. Platoon Training. R.D. [signature]	

D.A.G.
General Head Quarters.
3rd Echelon.
Base.
....

The War Diary of the battalion under my Coommand for the month of April 1917 is forwarded herewith please.

2nd ~~April~~ May 1917.

Lieut Colonel,
Commanding, 1st Bn; The Cameronians.

WAR DIARY of 1st Bn. The Cameronians

INTELLIGENCE SUMMARY

(Erase heading not required.)

Army Form C. 2118.

Place	Date	Hour	Summary of Events and Information	Remarks and references to Appendices
CAMPS	April 1st		Church Parade	
CORBIE	2nd		Battalion paraded 10 A.M. & marched to CORBIE (8 miles). Ate ruathe Officers own 25 left by train for ST POL	
BERTANGLES	3rd		Paraded 9.30 A.M. marched to BERTANGLES (13 miles)	
BEAUVAL	4th		Parade 9.20 A.M. marched to BEAUVAL (9 miles) Fronces hours. late Commando VIII Corps (pai heavy) inspected Battalion on march.	
LUCHEUX	5th		Parade 3.30 P.M. marched to LUCHEUX (9 miles). Division now in Third Army.	
	6th		Remained in LUCHEUX	
HUMBER-COURT	7th		Parade 9.30 A.M. marched to HUMBERCOURT (8 miles)	
BAILLEUVAL	8th		Parade 10 A.M. marched to BAILLEUVAL (4 miles). Three officers went up to reconnoitre ground near CROISELLES & the COJEUL River	

Army Form C. 2118.

WAR DIARY
or
INTELLIGENCE SUMMARY
(Erase heading not required.)

Instructions regarding War Diaries and Intelligence Summaries are contained in F. S. Regs., Part II. and the Staff Manual respectively. Title Pages will be prepared in manuscript.

Place	Date	Hour	Summary of Events and Information	Remarks and references to Appendices
BAILLEUVAL	April 9th		Remained in billets at BAILLEUVAL. Snowstorms during the day. Training in billets. News that THIRD Army attacked yesterday 6,100 prisoners.	
"	10th		H.Q. gun. Training in billets. Weather very bad.	
"			11.0am Prisoners taken by 3rd, 1st armies 11,000 guns.	
MERCATEL	11th		Marched to MERCATEL, leaving at 5.45 p.m., heavy snow, BEAUMETZ BLAIRVILLE & FEUTRON with Batln.	
HENIN	12th		C.O. reconnoitred ground as far as HENIN. Batln. marched to HENIN in N 33 C 9.0. took up position in sunken road in front of HENIN (30th Divn.) relieving 18th Northumberland Regt.	
	13th		A & B Coys moved forward to position in T 4.d.5.5. vacated by 21st Divn. which they moved forward to attack.	
	14th		A & B Coys moved forward and took up position for attack. The 14th Bde. were placed under orders of the 21st Divn.	

Place	Date	Hour	Summary of Events and Information	Remarks and references to Appendices
HINDENBURG LINE	April 14		The attack was made as under. A Coy attacked from HINDENBURG Front line Support line with 2 platoons in each. D Company in support to A. B Coy failed to get in the proper position C Coy therefore became the attacking Coy & took up position from the HINDENBURG Support line to a point 200x N. fit. At 5.30 a.m both companies went in but were held up in bn file lines by enemy bombardment. Actual ground gained was, in front line 150x, in support 100x. C Coy on left held up by M.G. fire. It formed them in Posn and raised were consolidated. Casualties Killed Capt. D FOSTER Wounded Capt. J BROWN Lieut. McFARLANE SLOAN (died of wounds) McGREGOR	

WAR DIARY or INTELLIGENCE SUMMARY

Army Form C. 2118.

Place	Date	Hour	Summary of Events and Information	Remarks and references to Appendices
H'burg Line	April 15th		Bombs etc. brought up preparatory to a further attack by 2 Coys.	
		4.15 am	At 4.15 am 2 Companies renewed attack down HINDENBURG Line. One Coy. in command of the attack on left support line failed to start at its correct time. This prevented the success of the operation. The attack down the front line got pushed back at dawn, but enemy to assist, of enemy rein(forcements) and bombs running short, we were driven back to the original position. 50 Bombers of Royal Welch Fusiliers were sent up to reinforce in H'burg front line.	
	17th		Battalion was relieved by the 1st Suffolks.	
	18th		Battalion in bivouac along HENIN-NEUVILLE VITASSE road N.32A & N.26D. Two companies up & masked in heavy traffic etc. ditto	
	19th		ditto	

WAR DIARY or INTELLIGENCE SUMMARY

Army Form C. 2118.

Place	Date	Hour	Summary of Events and Information	Remarks and references to Appendices
	April 20th		Relieved Middlesex Regt. in left Sub. Section. Bn H.Q. N.35.c.2.6. Digging of discommn. trenches continued.	
	21st		Quiet day.	
	22nd		Relieved by 2 Coys Middlesex & 2 Coys Argylls.	
	23rd		Attack by the 98th & 100th Bdes. 700 prisoners taken. Suffolks driven back to support position. 2 Coys (1 Argyle & 1 Middlesex) held out in a very advanced position.	
		At 2 P.M.	The Bn. moved up to a sunken road about T.3.A.	
			2 Coys carried bombs up for 98th Bde.	
		At 5 P.M.	Batln. moved up in support of 98th Bde.	
		At 6.24 p.m.	The 5th S.R. & R.W.F. attacked Front line coming under attacks of HINDENBURG support, attack failed.	
		11 p.m.	One Coy sent up to HINDENBURG line coming under orders of O.C. 4th Suffolks.	
			One Coy carrying up bombs to H'burg Support.	
			The Coy relieved 1 Coy on left of H'BURG Support.	
	24th		Coy on right of HINDENBURG line brought back where its Funnel	

Army Form C. 2118.

WAR DIARY
or
INTELLIGENCE SUMMARY
(Erase heading not required.)

Place	Date	Hour	Summary of Events and Information	Remarks and references to Appendices
	April 24 (cont)		Relief of 4th Suffolks in front position commenced finished by 8 p.m. Enemy reported to be retiring on left of HINDENBURG Suffat line. Patrol pushed forward down both front support line. Report that enemy had retired from those lines also. First position taken up on sunken road in Support line T.6.6.96. and 15c7 in front of Sunken road T.6.6.4.4. in front line. Posts made at T. c 2 points. 20th Royal Fusiliers on relieved on left. A boy brought back info received. 20 prisoners, 3 machine guns, 1 Trench mortar, 3 egg-exploders taken. 2 Coys 18th Middx. Pioneers dug trenches to protect left flank just N.E. of HINDENBURG Support from T.5.6.9.8. to T.6.6.3.0. - 4 Trenches dug Stokes by 4th Coy. Patrols in both lines of Sunken road also a second block in rear of front block made. And a block in tunnel in Suffat line.

WAR DIARY or INTELLIGENCE SUMMARY

Army Form C. 2118.

Place	Date	Hour	Summary of Events and Information	Remarks and references to Appendices
	April 25th		At dawn. A heavy recapture to trenches before Wancourt Ridge. Huffing sent in each day remainder of men in trenches.	
	26th		The Battn. relieved by 9th K.O.Y.L.I. (21st Div) & go to billets at BOIRY-BECQUERELLES.	
	27th		March to Huts at FICHEUX – 5 miles	
	28th & 29th		March to BAILLEULVAL 6 miles to billets, intensive training & all specialists etc.	
BAILLEULVAL			A draft of 130 O.R. arrived	
			Total casualties during the Four	
				Officers	O.R.
			Killed	2	34
			Missing	1	8
			Wounded	6	166
			not at duty	2	5
				10	213

[signature]

Lieut. Colonel
Commanding, 1st Bn. The Cameronians

Army Form C. 2118.

WAR DIARY or INTELLIGENCE SUMMARY

of 1/th 7th Camerons
(Several Rifles)

May 1917

Vol 34

30.M.
8 sheet
M.D.

Place	Date	Hour	Summary of Events and Information	Remarks and references to Appendices
BAILLEULVAL	1st		Training of battn. keen bomber etc continued	
MONCHY AU BOIS	2nd		Battn. marched to ADINFER WOOD aria. Bivuoaes amongst ruins of MONCHY-AU-BOIS	
"	3rd		Training of bombers. Lewis gunners etc continued	
"	4th		Training of bombers, Lewis gunners etc continued	
"	5th		Training continued	
"	6th		Morning Church Parade. Training continued in afternoon	
"	7th		Training continued	
"	8th		Training continued	
"	9th		Training continued	
"	10th		In Morning worked on a line of trenches, Communication with B. Scottish Rifles. Snipers worked at the Brigade School.	
"	11th		Training continued	
"	12th		Batt. marched to BOISLEUX ST MARC	

WAR DIARY
or
INTELLIGENCE SUMMARY
(Erase heading not required.)

Army Form C. 2118.

Place	Date	Hour	Summary of Events and Information	Remarks and references to Appendices
BOISLEUX ST MARC	17/3/17 13th		Morning - Church Parades. Training continued.	
	14th			
	15th	7.15 p.m.	At 7.15 P.M. the Battn. marched to CROISILLES and relieved the 2/Warwicks in a line of Posts in front of that village. A Battn. of the 162nd Divn. were on our Right and the 2/O&F.R. [?] were on the left. B Coln. to MOYENVILLE.	
From the	16th		Ammunition Patrols sent up to enemy wire, all fired on by sentries in spite of the fact that the division were trained with a belief that the enemy only held by a few men. Orders received for a company to be sent out to hold a reconnaissance in force & draw enemy fire. At 2 p.m. B Coy under Lt Sussex advanced in 2 lines widely extended from behind No's 1 & 2 Posts on left of CROISILLES - HENDECOURT Road. They advanced thirty in front of German wire without being fired on. At about 150x S.of my fire was opened on them by rifle & M.M. gun.	

WAR DIARY
or
INTELLIGENCE SUMMARY.

Army Form C. 2118.

Place	Date	Hour	Summary of Events and Information	Remarks and references to Appendices
Front Line	MAY 16		The Coy. Post came in at stand to and required out till dark when they withdrew. Information gained — Trench strongly held. Wire badly damaged. Casualties 5 killed, 6 missing, 15 wounded. Total 26 O.R.	
	17		The following wire was received from 33rd Divn. dated 17-5-17 "The information gained by reconnaissance part of the Cameronians yesterday is of greatest use to 15th Army. They make known to all O/Ps the G.O.C. 33rd Divn wishes to all O/Rs and men of 195 Inf Bde. He thanks the Cameronians for their sound work." A quiet day. A & D Coy each sent out a Patrol Party after dark with a view to getting a prisoner but no wires in man's Ed.	

Army Form C. 2118.

WAR DIARY
or
INTELLIGENCE SUMMARY.
(Erase heading not required.)

Instructions regarding War Diaries and Intelligence Summaries are contained in F. S. Regs., Part II. and the Staff Manual respectively. Title pages will be prepared in manuscript.

Place	Date May	Hour	Summary of Events and Information	Remarks and references to Appendices
Front line	18		Relieved by 2/ R.W.F. and moved back into shelters in sunken road at U.22.a.	
	19		Quiet day.	
	20		100 F. Bde. attacked H-Burg line at 5.15 a.m. Got first line but failed to get Sunken.	
		3 P.M.	O.C. about 3 P.M. received orders to move up to position of readiness in S. v. 1.3.d.	
			Moved up Sensée Valley by coys. in Artillery formation. Came under heavy Artillery fire. 2/Lt Scott (Adjt) severely wounded about 8 other casualties	
		5.20 P.M.	Received orders to attack H-Burg Support line in conjunction with 20 R.F. Our objective Nelly Lane to Oldenberg Lane Zero hour 7.30 p.m.	
		7.25 P.M.	Bn. advanced in 4 lines A & D Coys. Front lines B & C Coys. Rear lines	
			The 9/KLI had moved to our right but (?) did not materialise	

WAR DIARY
or
INTELLIGENCE SUMMARY.
(Erase heading not required.)

Army Form C. 2118.

Place	Date	Hour	Summary of Events and Information	Remarks and references to Appendices
Front Line	20	(cont.) Sunday	From the start the Batt. Intr. dura Fin and went too much to their left answer the line of the 20th R.F. The had at and they and the H-burg front line which was now Magmanite and from the barrage still in a line about 60× ahead. When it lifted they went on and 40 or 50 Germans rushed to them with hands up. The Cmys extended the bn. He. H-burg Support and reported accordingly. Jerry days in about 30× in front of it. Their position was so hard to locate that no mules (?) a ammunition could be sent up.	
	21		Reports received in morning showed that front of all 4 Coys were on a line between SENSÉE RIVER & FONTAINE Road about 50 yds from H-burg. Support. The day was fairly quiet except for paris her sniping and some M. gunnery from the H-burg support. At 11.30 p.m. the Batt. was relieved according to orders	

WAR DIARY
or
INTELLIGENCE SUMMARY.

Army Form C. 2118.

Place	Date	Hour	Summary of Events and Information	Remarks and references to Appendices
	21	(cont)	54 prisoners were taken by the Battn including 2 officers all of the 225th Regiment. (Prussians) Casualties. Killed d. wounded missing Officers 2/Lt T.A.Orr 2/Lt T.Scott (Adjt) 2/Lt Muir 2/Lt A.Phillips O.R. 14 100 16 Total 4 officers 130 O.ranks	
ST.LEGER	22		Battn. got in to trenches between 1 & 3 A.M. Lt.Col Chaplin D.S.O. resumed command.	
"	23		Rested, cleaned up & reorganised. Hun his usual A.itto.	
"	24		"	
"	25			
"	26		3rd Battn. ordered to take part in another attack on H-burg trench & line on the morning. moved up to the H-burg front line after quiet night in the Queens in before 13 officers 350 o.r. Strength of Battn. going up	

Army Form C. 2118.

WAR DIARY
or
INTELLIGENCE SUMMARY.
(Erase heading not required.)

Instructions regarding War Diaries and Intelligence Summaries are contained in F. S. Regs., Part II. and the Staff Manual respectively. Title pages will be prepared in manuscript.

Place	Date	Hour	Summary of Events and Information	Remarks and references to Appendices
Front Line	MAY 27 Sun		The Battn. got out into shell holes in front of the H-burg line before daylight and lay there till 1.55 p.m. when the attack commenced. The Battn. attacked on the left with 2/R.W.F on its right. Objective H-burg Support line from FONTAINE and to about 500 x S. The barrage which lasted 4 min. was weak and ragged. The Coys followed it up closely and got into the trench. B Coy went furthest & got into the barrage and had to come back. The Germans manned a freshed heavy m.g. and lifted which Coy filled B Coy to retire. The R.W.F. were held up on their right & B Coy also got into the trench up by pieces of wire and took C.P. into the trench. They retired when men were tired in the H-burg front line. Kay & A.m. till were tired in the H-burg front line. This was the third time B Coy had attacked in 10 days and although the men were worn out, their fighting spirit was apparent.	

Army Form C. 2118.

WAR DIARY
or
INTELLIGENCE SUMMARY.
(Erase heading not required.)

Instructions regarding War Diaries and Intelligence Summaries are contained in F. S. Regs., Part II. and the Staff Manual respectively. Title pages will be prepared in manuscript.

Place	Date	Hour	Summary of Events and Information	Remarks and references to Appendices
Front line	May 28		The Battn. were relieved by 12/ Queens Regt. after the Hy. came down to huts in MOYENVILLE.	
			Casualties Killed — three	
			Wounded — Capt. KENNEDY, 2Lt. FORBES, 2Lt. CLARKE — 7	2
			Lieut. CRAIG, 2Lt. TAYLOR	46
			Missing — 2Lieut. NEWLANDS	24
				72
			Total Officers – 6, O.R. –	
MOYENVILLE	29		Rest in huts.	
"	30		Marched at 5 P.M. to BAILLEULVAL — 8 mile	
BAILLEULVAL	31		Rest. Clean up.	
			Total ration strength 40 O.R.	K. W. M.
				3 1 — = 10 Officers
				6 146 40 = 202 O.R.
				16

W.K.Smith for Lieut Colonel
Comdg. 1/12. 76 Camerounams

SECRET.

D.A.G.
    General Headquarters.
        3rd Echelon. Base.
        ....

    The War Diary of the battalion under my command for the month of June is forwarded herewith please.

In the Field.
1st July 1917.

                Major,
Commanding, 1st Battalion The Cameronians.

Agent

WAR DIARY of 1st Battalion
or
INTELLIGENCE SUMMARY 7th Camerons
June 1917

Seaforth R.H.
Vol 33

81.11.
5 sheets

Place	Date June 1917	Hour	Summary of Events and Information	Remarks and references to Appendices
BAILLEULVAL	1st		Musketry, coy & platoon drill, specialist training	
"	2nd		Inspection by G.O.C. Corps.	
"	3rd	Sun	Church parades.	
"	4		Musketry, coys platoon drill, specialist training	
"	5		ditto	
"	6		} Inspection of transport by C.O.	
"	7		Musketry, coy & platoon drill, specialist training	
"	8		} Weather very hot but dry	
"	9		Route march.	
"	10	Sun	Church parades.	
"	11		Wet morning. Training in billets.	
"	12		2 Coys. Tactical scheme. 1 coy range. 1 coy training	
"	13		ditto	
"	14			
"	15		Bn. sham fight, rapid wiring, training assembly	

WAR DIARY
or
INTELLIGENCE SUMMARY.
(Erase heading not required.)

Army Form C. 2118.

Place	Date JUNE 1917	Hour	Summary of Events and Information	Remarks and references to Appendices
BAILLEULVAL	16		Battalion Sports.	
"	17 Sun.		Brigade Church parade. Sir D.C. SNOW, Commanding VII CORPS. presented Medal Ribbons to Officers & men of the brigade.	
MOYENVILLE	18		The Battn. marched at 6.30 a.m. to Camp at MOYENVILLE. Weather extremely hot.	
MOYENVILLE	19		Moved up in the evening to Trenches assunken road behind CROISILLES. Relieved 6th Leicester, 21st Divn. in support to first line. Officers visited the front line with view to be made at end of week.	
CROISILLES	20		Remained in Support. No shelling. 50 men working in communication trenches each night.	
"	21			
"	22		H.Q. moved up into tunnel in The Quarry at 6 p.m. A & B Coys. under Capt Wright moved up into LUMP LANE before midnight. 1 Coy 18th Middlesex Pioneers also arrived in LUMP LANE. ½ C Coy moved up in to the Quarry in Support.	
"	23		The Objective was to capture and consolidate TUNNEL Trench establishing a block in it 160x from LUMP LANE. Zero hour was fixed at 12 midnight.	

WAR DIARY or INTELLIGENCE SUMMARY

Army Form C. 2118.

Place	Date	Hour	Summary of Events and Information	Remarks and references to Appendices
CROISILLES	JUNE 24 1917	5 a.m.	At Zero a barrage was put on Tunnel Trench. At Zero+1 it commenced to creep at 25 yds a minute back to OLDENBURG LANE where it remained for 12 hours. At Zero+1 the Coys began to advance. They were fired on almost at once by 1 or 2 machine guns and the outer platoons were shelled by being held up by some wire from behind which they continued to advance but Germans in shell holes. Jo front platoon continued to advance but finding the outer platoons had stopped to the officers being wounded they fell back again. the centre platoon lay in where they were. Pioneers joined up the trench into LUMP LANE. the Germans put up a truck on the bank of M/G Platoon from the captured trench. At dawn they were as possible from the Coys were withdrawn to CROISILLES to 2/5 R.F. having taken over LUMP LANE. Between 6 & 7 p.m. the Battn was relieved by 1/9 H.L.I. (10th Bde) and marched back to Camp at MAYENVILLE.	
			Casualties killed — Lt. MURRAY wounded — 2Lt. CARTWRIGHT (at duty) killed — 3Lt. HOURSTON wounded other ranks — 6 / 32 Total 38	
MAYENVILLE	25		Rested and cleaned up.	

Army Form C. 2118.

WAR DIARY
or
INTELLIGENCE SUMMARY.
(Erase heading not required.)

Instructions regarding War Diaries and Intelligence Summaries are contained in F. S. Regs., Part II. and the Staff Manual respectively. Title pages will be prepared in manuscript.

Place	Date JUNE	Hour 1917	Summary of Events and Information	Remarks and references to Appendices
MOYENVILLE	26		Coy. drill, mainly specialist instruction. A draft of 2 Officers and 79 other ranks arrived.	
"	27		Drill mostly in the entire	
"	28			
"	29		The Batt. marched to MONCHY-au-BOIS at 5 p.m. and billeted in the town there.	
MONCHY	30		All companies church digging	

W.C.J. Smith
Maj.
Commanding the The Cameronian

CONFIDENTIAL.

D.A.G.
    General Head Quarters.
        3rd Echelon   Base.

    The War Diary of the battalion under my command for the month of July 1917, is forwarded herewith please.

31st July 1917.
                                      Lieut Colonel,
                Commanding, 1st Bn: The Cameronians.

Army Form C. 2118.

July 1917 WAR DIARY of 1st Battalion
INTELLIGENCE SUMMARY. 7h Cameronians (Sco. Rifles)
(Erase heading not required.)

Place	Date	Hour	Summary of Events and Information	Remarks and references to Appendices
MONCHY au BOIS	July 1st		Church Parades	
LEALVILLERS	2nd		marched to LEALVILLERS. About 13 miles. Press starting point 9.30 A.M. Halfway halt for dinner at 11.50 A.M. March resumed 1.30 P.M. Arrived 4.30 P.M. Packs were carried for men.	
NAOURS	3rd		Marched to NAOURS 12½ miles. Parade 7.12 – Press starting point 8.12. Men in full marching order. Very hot. Apprecive day- hem very soft – 187 men fell out, chiefly owing to heat although there were a good many cases of sore feet. Arrived 1.15 P.M.	
BOUCHON	4th		Marched to BOUCHON, 11 miles. Parade 5.30 A.M. March broke– Arrived 10.20 A.M.	
CONDE	5th		Marched to CONDE. Parade 5.30 A.M. Arrived 8 A.M. Billets good with plenty of room.	
	6th		Men cleaning up. Lectures.	

Army Form C. 2118.

WAR DIARY
or
INTELLIGENCE SUMMARY
(Erase heading not required.)

Instructions regarding War Diaries and Intelligence Summaries are contained in F.S. Regs., Part II. and the Staff Manual respectively. Title Pages will be prepared in manuscript.

Place	Date	Hour	Summary of Events and Information	Remarks and references to Appendices
CONDE	July 7th		Route march from 6.30 A.M. – 8 for men who fell out on July 3rd. Physical Drill 7 – 7.30 for remainder.	
		9.10	Bombing – Bayonet fighting. C.O. Instructs Captains. Handling Arms. Officials at training.	
		10.15	Draft 6 Officers and 239 O.R. Nearly all men who had been in France or Salonica before, & belonging to 1st, 2nd, 5th, 6th, 9th, 10th or 16th Bn. A good draft.	
	July 8th		Church Parade. C.O. instructs 1 draft at 2 P.M.	
	July 9th	6 – 7.30	Rifle & wheeled draft. Route march for men who fell out.	
		8.30 – 9.50	Bombing – Bayonet fighting. Rifles firing officials at training.	
		9.10 – 10	Battery Parades.	

2449 Wt. W14957/M90 750,000 1/16 J.B.C. &/A: Forms/C.2118/12.

WAR DIARY
or
INTELLIGENCE SUMMARY

Army Form C. 2118.

Place	Date	Hour	Summary of Events and Information	Remarks and references to Appendices
CONDÉ	July 11		The Battalion had use of Brigade Training Ground. Parade 8 A.M. Artillery formation were practised. Platoon & Company Drill. Marched back by BETTENCOURT & LONG PRÉ. Bathing Parade.	
	July 12	8.30 - 9.30	Other Company on Range.	
		9 to 12	Bombing, Bayonet Fighting. Rapid firing, 20 minutes each. Musketry - Platoon Drill - Handy Arms. Ceremonial Drill. These did not kneel.	
	July 13	6 A.M	Route march to view the path cut on July 2nd. 1 Company Range. Remainder as above.	
	July 13	6.30 1.30	Brigade Route march. LONGPRÉ - BETTENCOURT - BREWERY - CONDÉ Range. Khaki as Inhabitant.	

Army Form C. 2118.

WAR DIARY
or
INTELLIGENCE SUMMARY

(Erase heading not required.)

Instructions regarding War Diaries and Intelligence Summaries are contained in F. S. Regs., Part II. and the Staff Manual respectively. Title Pages will be prepared in manuscript.

Place	Date	Hour	Summary of Events and Information	Remarks and references to Appendices
JULY CONDE	14		Training. Knock out competition in range	
"	15 Sunday		Church Parade.	
"	16		Training. Company & Platoon drill.	
"	17		ditto	
"	18		Battn. paraded at 7.15 AM. and marched to Divl. Horse Show near CAVILLON. Marched back again at 6.30 p.m.	
"	19		Marched to Bde. Training ground at RIVIERE. Practised Coy. drill and advance under a barrage represented by flags.	
"	20		Training, musketry, Coy & platoon drill.	
"	21		Training, musketry, etc.	
"	22 Sun.		Church parade	
"	23		Battn. Aquatic Sports held in the river by the Rwere Somme.	

2449 Wt. W14957/M90 750,000 1/16 J.B.C. & A. Forms/C.2118/12.

Army Form C. 2118.

WAR DIARY
or
INTELLIGENCE SUMMARY

(Erase heading not required.)

Instructions regarding War Diaries and Intelligence Summaries are contained in F.S. Regs., Part II. and the Staff Manual respectively. Title Pages will be prepared in manuscript.

Place	Date 1917 July	Hour	Summary of Events and Information	Remarks and references to Appendices
CONDÉ	25		Training continuing. First day of Base Boxing tournament.	
"	26		" Regimental concert.	
"	27		Route march	
"	28		Training continuing	
"	29	Sun.	Church parades	
"	30		Battn. route march, L'ETOILE, LONG.	
"	31		Battn. (less A Coy) paraded at 3.30 P.M. and marched to PONT REMY Station (about 7 miles) to entrain for DUNKERQUE. The Division moves to join XV Corps, First Army.	

31st July 1917.

[signature] Lieut. Colonel
[signature] Commanding.

WAR DIARY of 1st Battalion The Cameronians (Scottish Rifles)

Army Form C. 2118.

August 1917

Place	Date	Hour	Summary of Events and Information	Remarks and references to Appendices
BRAY DUNES	1		The Battn (less A Coy) with Transport E arrived by train at DUNKERQUE at 6 A.M. and detrained by the harbour. A pouring wet morning. Marched out to huts at BRAY DUNES distance 7 miles. The men were taken to troops.	
	2		1st Trans. Int. moved by road. X Corps HQ also in BRAY DUNES. The division is in Corps Reserve. Huts from Sergeons to the sea being held by 66th & 49th Divns.	
	3		A Coy arrived about 10 a.m. A wet day.	
	4		Some training attempted. Weather still continues.	
	5	Sun	Training, musketry, extended order formations etc.	
	6		Church parades.	

VA 37

Army Form C. 2118.

WAR DIARY
or
INTELLIGENCE SUMMARY

(Erase heading not required.)

Instructions regarding War Diaries and Intelligence Summaries are contained in F.S. Regs., Part II. and the Staff Manual respectively. Title Pages will be prepared in manuscript.

Place	Date	Hour	Summary of Events and Information	Remarks and references to Appendices
BRAY DUNES	6th		Training. Company Drill - musketry. Attack Speakers training in afternoon. Officers & NCO's under R.S.M. Rising school for Officers in evening	
	7th		Brigade Route march BRAY DUNES - along South side of Canal ZUYDCOOTE - Sands - Camp - Specialist training: Rising School.	
	8th		Company Drill - musketry - Reconnoitering Patrols. Truck to Trench attack - Specialist Training & Rising School -	
	9th		Range firing & Attack movements. 2/Lt. A.C. Price killed by burst hurled for Athern in front line and Drummer	

2/Lt A.C. Price killed by burst hurled for Athern in front line and Drummer

2449 Wt. W14957/M90 750,000 1/16 J.B.C. & A. Forms/C.2118/12.

WAR DIARY
or
INTELLIGENCE SUMMARY
(Erase heading not required.)

Army Form C. 2118.

Place	Date	Hour	Summary of Events and Information	Remarks and references to Appendices
BRAY DUNES	Aug 10th		Route march. BRAY DUNES - SEA SHORE - ZUYDCOOTE STN - main roads S of DUNKERQUE CANAL - BRAY DUNES STN - CAMP.	
"	11th		Special it Training & Rifle on Range. Gun Companies on Range - Gun Companies Wiring & Revetting with Lewis-Coy. Company Drill.	
"	12th Sun		Church Parade. Battalion took on Coast Defence BRAY DUNES Area.	
	13th		Training. Company drill - Bayonet Fighting - Rapid loading.	
	14th		Training, etc.	
COXYDE	15th		The Battn. marched in the early morning march to COXYDE.	

August 1917

WAR DIARY of 1st Battalion The Connaught (Southern Irish Rifle)

INTELLIGENCE SUMMARY.

Army Form C. 2118.

(Erase heading not required.)

Instructions regarding War Diaries and Intelligence Summaries are contained in F. S. Regs., Part II. and the Staff Manual respectively. Title pages will be prepared in manuscript.

Place	Date 1917	Hour	Summary of Events and Information	Remarks and references to Appendices
Trenches	16		On night 16/17 The Battn. relieved 1/5 The Rs West Riding Regt 32nd Divn	
			in Reserve trench N. of NIEUPORT. Relief was complete by 11 p.m.	
			There was no shelling.	
			Bn HQ at M.21.G.4.7 450 yds M. of LOMBARTZIDE 1.20 p.m.	
"	17		Transport remained near COXYDE. Went to ration trucks	
"	18		Light shelling, working parties under RE	
"	19		Q certain amount of shelling by field guns & 5.9 hows with	
"	20		few wounded & infantry of gas shells.	
			Lost a Lieutenant shelling	
			Shelling heavy, shelling of Lannes line from front line 1 man killed, 2 wounded.	
"	21		As above, enemy put over a quantity of gas shells in the night.	
"	22		Relieved by 2/R.W.F. in front line after dark	
			The relief was hardly complete when the enemy attacked on four posts	
			after heavy shelling. Hand to hand fighting took place, the enemy eventually	
			retired.	
"	23		To Britt 8th GeLEIDE post recaptured.	

WAR DIARY
or
INTELLIGENCE SUMMARY

Army Form C. 2118.

Place	Date	Hour	Summary of Events and Information	Remarks and references to Appendices
Trenches	Dec 2nd		A highly successful raid was carried out by B Coy under command of Capt Surus. Objective being German P.O.s about M.22.c.2.7. The raiding party consisting of 3 officers & 88 men and was divided into 4 parties. At 10.15 p.m. the barrage opened and the attacking parties advanced. The main party (Lt. Mc.Arthur & 30 men) were fired on by a machine gun but killed all its crew & pushed on to their objective which they failed to recognise. At M.21.b.9.8. they ran into another party, whom they killed 6 bar one. The occupants of concealed M.G. section were all killed, but all were not found. A garrison of 40 men was left in the post. Our casualties were 5 O.R. wounded. Prisoner taken were 1 officer (unh) Lieut Emil & 8 unwounded. 1 M. Gun was taken. At least 20 Germans were killed. The G.O.C. 3rd Divn sent a wire of congratulations, also the G.O.C. XV Corps.	

Army Form C. 2118.

WAR DIARY
or
INTELLIGENCE SUMMARY.
(Erase heading not required.)

Instructions regarding War Diaries and Intelligence Summaries are contained in F. S. Regs., Part II. and the Staff Manual respectively. Title pages will be prepared in manuscript.

Place	Date	Hour	Summary of Events and Information	Remarks and references to Appendices
Nieuport	25		At 9.25 P.M. the S.O.S. signal went up from our advanced position. The artillery at once opened fire. B Coy supported by C Coy & 2 Coys 2nd R.F. held on as long as possible but after heavy fighting were forced to retire. They fell back to the positions originally held by us on the 23rd inst. Capt Seaver was unfortunately killed by a shell whilst arranging a counter attack. Casualties:— 2 killed — Capt Seaver, Pte Martin 16 wounded 8 missing	
Trenches	26		C company relieved B company in the front line. B Coy went into reserve in the REDAN.	
Trenches	27		The Battalion was relieved by 15th H.L.I. and moved back to OOST DUNKERQUE for breakfast and then on to LA PANNE to billets	
LA PANNE	28th			
LA PANNE	29th		The Battalion moved by bus to CAPELLE to billets arriving thereabout 11.15 am. Transport went by road.	
CAPELLE	30		Cleaning up and checking deficiencies. Orders for move to MOULLE area received	

Army Form C. 2118.

WAR DIARY
or
INTELLIGENCE SUMMARY.
(Erase heading not required.)

Instructions regarding War Diaries and Intelligence Summaries are contained in F. S. Regs., Part II. and the Staff Manual respectively. Title pages will be prepared in manuscript.

Place	Date	Hour	Summary of Events and Information	Remarks and references to Appendices
CAPPELLE	31.		The Battalion marched to PETITE SYNTHE and there entrained proceeding by bus to MOULLE. Transport went by road leaving at 9am and arriving at MOULLE about 5pm.	

Cmdg. 1/Bn. The Queens
Lieut. Colonel
1/9/17

Secret

Army Form C. 2118

WAR DIARY of 1st Bn. T.R.E. Cameronians

INTELLIGENCE SUMMARY.
(Erase heading not required.)

Vol 38

Instructions regarding War Diaries and Intelligence Summaries are contained in F. S. Regs., Part II. and the Staff Manual respectively. Title pages will be prepared in manuscript.

Place	Date	Hour	Summary of Events and Information	Remarks and references to Appendices
MOULLE	Sept 1917 1st		Cleaning up after coming out of line	
	2nd		Church Parade. Baths.	
	3rd		Training. Drill - Rifle loading. Bayonet Fighting.	
	4th		Route march. EPERLECQUES - OUEST MONT - EST MONT - GANSPETTE - MOULLE - MOULLE	
	5th		Training. 1 Company on 30 yards Range. Running Long Drill - Bayonet Fighting - Rifle Loading - musketry. Companies marched independently to a Training Area. At times manoeuvre - Trench to Trench Attack. Attack in Strong Point by Platoons were practised.	
	6th 12.30		Companies marched out to Training Area. Attack by Platoon of Strong Points.	Ashley Jameson
	7th		Training over Rifle. Company Drill. musketry. Bayonet fighting.	
	8th		Church Parade. Battn. Officers went up to reconnoitre to line	
	9th		front near ZILLEBEKE.	

Army Form C. 2118.

WAR DIARY
or
INTELLIGENCE SUMMARY.
(Erase heading not required.)

Instructions regarding War Diaries and Intelligence Summaries are contained in F. S. Regs., Part II. and the Staff Manual respectively. Title pages will be prepared in manuscript.

Place	Date	Hour	Summary of Events and Information	Remarks and references to Appendices
MOULLE	Sept 10th		All companies on Range. Practice was much the same. 5 rounds 200x. Slow. 5 rounds. Rapid 10 rounds. 60 rounds all round at 300x. Shooting fair. Lewis gun practice at full and plate afterwards.	
	11th		Brigade Route march	
			WESTROVE - EPERLEQUES - MOULLE - MOULLE	
	12th		Battalion on "A" Training Area. Attack practice by Coys. Same afterwards by the Battalion.	
	13th		Training near Bn HQ - Range	
	14th		Sick - Mopped up things - briefing	
	15th		Marched from MOULLE to LEDERZEELE area	
	16th		Marched to STEENVOORDE area	
	17th		Marched to THIESHOUK area	
	18th		Inspections + Anti-gas training	
	20th		Marched to THUNDERER CAMP, near WESTOUTRE	

Army Form C. 2118.

WAR DIARY
or
INTELLIGENCE SUMMARY.
(Erase heading not required.)

Instructions regarding War Diaries and Intelligence Summaries are contained in F. S. Regs., Part II. and the Staff Manual respectively. Title pages will be prepared in manuscript.

Place	Date	Hour	Summary of Events and Information	Remarks and references to Appendices
20-24			Remained in Camp at WESTOUTRE	
	24th		Marched to CANAL Dugouts in BEDFORD HOUSE AREA.	
	25th		On evening 25th moved forward and dug in in new positions in vicinity of STIRLING CASTLE	
	26th	4 AM	General situation good. All Companies have moved forward. A Coy to support 4th Kings At B Coy to support & reinforce 2nd Queens W. Surry. C + D Coys to reserve positions about 100 yds West of INVERNESS COPSE	
		11 AM	B Coy stormed an enemy strong point killing 16 other ranks and 4 officers & capturing 24 other ranks + 2 officers.	
		6 PM	Enemy counterattacked heavily from S.E. direction (from GHELUVELT). Our Artillery barrage very fine	

WAR DIARY or INTELLIGENCE SUMMARY

Army Form C. 2118.

Place	Date	Hour	Summary of Events and Information	Remarks and references to Appendices
	26th	6 p.m.	Enemy Counter attack a failure.	
		6/2 p.m.	C & D Coys moved from position to form a strong point astride the MENIN ROAD, N.W. of INVERNESS COPSE.	
	27th		Battalion moved by companies to positions in the vicinity of STIRLING CASTLE & TAN 16 PPRE. Enemy shelling heavy.	
	28th		Battalion relieved by 8th Yorks & Lancs on morning of 28th. Marched to No 1 Camp Château Area at DICKEBUSCH. Enemy shelling in the H.V. area caused three for the night.	
			Guns & aeroplanes bombs the camp. 1 man wounds.	
RECKINGHEM	29th		Marched to PENINGHEIST & entrained & detrained at REBLINGHEM & marched to RECKINGHEM arriving at 8 p.m. Casualties in the line were 1 Officer (Lt. A Cornwall 1st O.R.) killed, wounded & missing. 3/Lt Man A.K. was Left 2/Lieut 2/Lt Walker, Chambers & Roahm.	

Army Form C. 2118.

WAR DIARY
or
INTELLIGENCE SUMMARY.
(Erase heading not required.)

Place	Date	Hour	Summary of Events and Information	Remarks and references to Appendices
RECKING HPR			The but wounded.	
			Clearing up of the enemy out of trins. Inspection etc.	
			R. S Hunter buy	
			Com. F 1st Bde the Camerarans	

1923

Covel

WAR DIARY of 1st Battalion The (Queen's Own) Royal
INTELLIGENCE SUMMARY — (Scottish Rifles).

Vol 39

35 M
4 wheels

Place	Date	Hour	Summary of Events and Information	Remarks and references to Appendices
RACQUINGHEM	1917 Oct 1st		Cleaning up. Battalion ceremonial Drill.	
	2nd		Brigade practice for C-in-C's Inspection in field NE BLARINGHEM.	
	3rd		C-in-C's Inspection of 19th Brigade. After inspection Battalion marched back in Column of Route.	
	4th		Training. Physical Training. Bayonet Fighting. Company Drill.	
	5th		Training Drill, musketry. Bayonet fighting.	
	6th		Specialist Training in the afternoon. Battalion paraded at 5.20 A.M. and marched to rly. Training Area. Billets at MORNINGHEM. Arrived 11.45 AM.	
MORNINGHEM	7th		Distance about 14 miles. In evening Company moved to farms by train went by to BAILLEUL arr. left MORNINGHEM 10.15 AM, detrained at WIZERNES 1 P.M. arr in BAILLEUL 10 P.M. moved to BULFORD CAMP nr NEUVE EGLISE. Transport by road.	
	9th		COs Company Commanders reconnoitre line E of MESSINES. Transport arrived in afternoon.	

WAR DIARY
or
INTELLIGENCE SUMMARY.

Army Form C. 2118.

Place	Date	Hour	Summary of Events and Information	Remarks and references to Appendices
LINE	9th		Battalion handed 7.15 A.M. marched to BRISTOL CASTLE & relieved 2nd Bucks L.I. Paraded in evening with 4 5Ph	
	10th		marched up to line and relieved 9th Rifle Brigade. Quiet day. Some shelling round Reserve Coy. Trench huts	
	11th		Fired from KINGSCLERE. Agent on my foot. line near WINDMILL. Another quiet day. Aeroplane dropped bomb near Bn H.Q. and a certain amount of shelling at night & early morning	
	12th		near Bn H.Q. Support Company heavily shelled about 10 P.M. Retaliation called for & given with good effect. Enemy trench mortar plus in no front line near WINDMILL & lines heavy on our trenches. Relieved by 1st MIDDLESEX Killing 3 men.	
BRISTOL CASTLE	13th		Moved BRISTOL CASTLE 6.A.M. men cleaning up & in a morile [?]	
	14th		Working parties. Relieved at BRISTOL CASTLE by 1st Queens, but March to camp near NEUVE EGLISE (ALDERSHOT CAMP)	

Army Form C. 2118.

WAR DIARY
or
INTELLIGENCE SUMMARY.
(Erase heading not required.)

Instructions regarding War Diaries and Intelligence Summaries are contained in F. S. Regs., Part II. and the Staff Manual respectively. Title pages will be prepared in manuscript.

Place	Date	Hour	Summary of Events and Information	Remarks and references to Appendices
ALDERSHOT CAMP	15th		Cleaning up and inspection	
	16th		Training from 9 – 12. Working parties	
YPRES	17th		Battalion paraded at 11 A.m. & went by bus to YPRES. Transport left 9.30 by road. Arrived in new Camp nr. YPRES about 2 P.m.	
	18th		Whole Battalion out working under Canadian & 1st Rly Coy.	
	19th		11.30 – 7½ 11 A.m. – 5 P.m. 200 men in morning & 200 in afternoon out working. Whole Battalion out from 8.30 A.m. to 4 P.m.	
	20th			
	21st		Day spent in improving Camp. No working parties were required. Working parties for the full Railway & Entrenchments out in morning and 2 in afternoon. Heavy snowflakes &c.	
	22nd		Heavy aeroplane raid over about 9 P.m. Several bombs dropped near the Camp. Men were killed and 5 wounded. Working parties no. for 22nd = Day Work Party Camp in a Fray	
	23rd		Last note – a large number of men sick in severe epidemic	

Army Form C. 2118.

Army Form C. 2118.

WAR DIARY
or
INTELLIGENCE SUMMARY.
(Erase heading not required.)

Place	Date	Hour	Summary of Events and Information	Remarks and references to Appendices
YPRES	Oct 24th		Battalion left YPRES, relieved by 16 K.R.R. went back to NEUVE EGLISE in buses.	
NEUVE EGLISE	25		Inspection of Clothing & etc. hut cleaning up. Battn got Prot. maw awarded D.S.O.	
	26		Training. In vicinity and practising revetting trench Ypres. Shot stammy in attacking an above.	
	27		Church Parades.	
	28		Training.	
	29		Training. 5th. Hus. hdly. Boy. not fighting.	
	30		Win's revetting French. Battalion went in to live relieving 4th Kings in the right sub sector near MES	
	31st		Trenches.	

Commanding, 1st Battalion The Cameronians.
Lieut. Colonel.

1st November 1914

Army Form C. 2118.

WAR DIARY of 1st Bn. The Cameronians (Scottish Rifles)

INTELLIGENCE SUMMARY.

(Erase heading not required.)

VIII 40

Place	Date	Hour	Summary of Events and Information	Remarks and references to Appendices
LINE	Nov 1st		Battalion in line in front of WARNETON (MESSINES SECTOR)	
			"B" Echelon PENZANCE LINES 2/Lt PRESTON wounded	
	2nd		Quiet day on the whole	
	3rd			
	4th		Battalion moved back into Support near BRISTOL CASTLE	
			Casualties whilst in the line 1 O.R. killed 18 wounded	
BRISTOL	5th		Working parties and night digging new support line	
CASTLE			Lt CLAY joined the battalion	
	6th		Working parties. 2 O.R. wounded	
	7th		Battalion relieved by 2nd Bn Worcestershire Regt. and	
			moved back to CANTEEN CORNER CAMP, arr. in by 11.35 P.M.	
CANTEEN	8th		Bn. Cleaning up. Battn. Inspection	
CORNER	9th		Training	
CAMP	10th		Training	
	11th		Training	
	12th		Training 2/Lts Anderson & Kirkpatrick joined the Battalion	

Army Form C. 2118.

WAR DIARY
or
INTELLIGENCE SUMMARY.
(Erase heading not required.)

Instructions regarding War Diaries and Intelligence Summaries are contained in F. S. Regs., Part II. and the Staff Manual respectively. Title pages will be prepared in manuscript.

Place	Date	Hour	Summary of Events and Information	Remarks and references to Appendices
CANTEEN CNR			Training	
CNVER	14th		Left CANTEEN CORNER & marched to STRAZEELE en route to YPRES. Division relieved by 5th Australian Divs.	
	15th		Remained at STRAZEELE	
	16th		Battalion left by Bus and went to YPRES marching from the to ???? MENIN ROAD AREA	
MENIN ROAD	17th		Infantry camp	
	18th		2/Lt Lt J.G. Chaplin who has been in command France with the Battalion since August 1914 & in command since May 1915 hands over command of 10th R.S. 3rd Division to Major C.C. Fish on command of the Battalion.	
POTIJZE	19th		Changed camps the Menin Road camp heavily shelled. New camp in POTIJZE AREA.	
	20th		Cleaning up new camp. Manning & making improvements. Some shells	

Army Form C. 2118.

WAR DIARY
or
INTELLIGENCE SUMMARY.
(Erase heading not required.)

Place	Date	Hour	Summary of Events and Information	Remarks and references to Appendices
POTIJZE	Nov 22nd			
	23rd		Battalion paraded at 2.30 and marched up to SUPPORT in relief of 4 SUFFOLKS. Shelling was heavy during relief but not many casualties. 2 Companies at ABRAHAM HEIGHTS, 2 Coy at HAMBURG (Bn HQ at CREST FARM). B Coy to ROET HOEK, D Coy to POTIJZE.	
	24th		Battalion moved up to the line in relief of 1st & 2nd Argylls. Line had between PASSCHENDAELE section. Before relief shelling very heavy but quietened down. There was considerable 2 Companies in front line, 1 Coy CREST FARM SUPPORT, 1 Coy HQ HILLSIDE FM. Enemy aircraft very active but relief was normal. Enemy shelled during night.	
	25th		At times shelling very heavy during the day. Enemy aircraft flew very low during the day fire directed to harass from 12 - 4. They shortly found the position of our posts in front were subjected to to very heavy shelling during the rest of the Battalion frontage in the line	

WAR DIARY
INTELLIGENCE SUMMARY

Army Form C. 2118.

Place	Date	Hour	Summary of Events and Information	Remarks and references to Appendices
	Nov 25		At 7 p.m. shelling was rather heavy & S.O.S. was sent up from somewhere on the right of the Battalion. Our barrage came down almost at once and the enemy very shortly after. The shelling was intense. Enemy barrage chiefly on CREST FM Ridge. In Coy there lost very heavily. 1 Officer (Capt Potts) killed, 3 Offrs shell shock. 1 O.R. killed, 30 O.R. wounded. Shelling continued to be heavy. During the rest of the night	
	26th		Shelling all day heavy around CREST FARM & in PASSCHENDAELE. In the afternoon the Coy at CREST FARM were moved behind the Crest in order to lessen casualties. Enemy Aircraft again very active. Our front line posts and Company at white PASSCHENDAELE heavily shelled throughout the Casualties were not heavy. Shelling again heavy throughout the day. The day was wet and the ground was	
	27th		before. Machine Gun fire was hot indeed. 1 Lgt & 2nd Ft relieved by Cny/R.W.F Battalion relieved by 2 nd R.W.Fusiliers & sent back to Support. 3 Coys at HAMBURG & 1 Coy ABRAHAM HEIGHTS	

WAR DIARY
or
INTELLIGENCE SUMMARY.
(Erase heading not required.)

Army Form C. 2118.

Place	Date	Hour	Summary of Events and Information	Remarks and references to Appendices
HAMBURG	28th		It was very dark about 6.15 P.M. S.O.S. sent up from the Right Battalion in front line. There was no attack but everyone was put down by Enemy following up our attack about 3/4 hour later. Enemy's barrage of our line for 2/1/2 hrs was at times very heavy.	
	29th		Battalion relieved by 16th K.R.R. & went back to camp here. Lt. JEAN Crudlett was hit in his 3 wounds: 12.4 O.C. Killed + wounded.	
	30th		Lft Pt JEAN by train & went back to camp at R.R. AND HOEK	

O. Scott Major
Commanding 1st Battalion The Cameronians

Secret

WAR DIARY of 1st Battalion the Cambrians (Scottish Rifles)
or
~~INTELLIGENCE SUMMARY~~ for December 1917.

Army Form C. 2118.

(Erase heading not required.)

Instructions regarding War Diaries and Intelligence Summaries are contained in F. S. Regs., Part II. and the Staff Manual respectively. Title pages will be prepared in manuscript.

Place	Date	Hour	Summary of Events and Information	Remarks and references to Appendices
BRANDHOEK	DEC 1st		Battn in cleaning. Inspection of Equipment & clothing. Baths	
	2nd		Training Bayonet Fighting. Drill	
	3rd		Training	
	4th		Training	
ST JEAN	5th		Battalion left ST LAWRENCE CAMP and marched to ST JEAN (DIV SUPPORT)	M.O.
	6th		Battalion on working parties of 400 men under RE on plank roads near ABRAAM HEIGHTS.	
			Working parties as above	
	7th		D. ts	
	8th		D. ts	
	9th		D. ts	
	10th		Battalion entrained at ST JEAN Station & arrived at	
WATTOO			AREELS from there marched to billets in WATTOO area. Billets very scattered.	3 sheets
			General up. Inspection	

Army Form C. 2118.

WAR DIARY
or
INTELLIGENCE SUMMARY.
(Erase heading not required.)

Instructions regarding War Diaries and Intelligence Summaries are contained in F. S. Regs., Part II. and the Staff Manual respectively. Title pages will be prepared in manuscript.

Place	Date	Hour	Summary of Events and Information	Remarks and references to Appendices
WATOU	Dec 12		Training. 1 Company route march inspected by C.O before moving off	
			Remainder of Companies Drill, Bayonet Fighting	
	13		Training on Ranges. Ranges shortly to be moved	
	14		One Company route march & bayonet or range. Remaining Companies Drill, Bayonet Fighting, musketry	
	15		Training in above	
	16		Training	
	17		Training	
	18		Training. Lecture to Government R.O. 11/8 by Division Commander on Battle of CAMBRAI	
	19		Training	
	20		Training	
	21st		Battalion left WATOU AREA marched to ABEELE Sidings entrained at YPRES TRIANGLEY marched to camp at SPOIL VATION	
			GEN.RN.SR. in rel of 16 to 16 K.R.R.	
	22nd		Working parties under 8th Bn R.E on flank roads. 3	

D. D. & L., London, E.C. (A.7883) Wt. W803/M1672 350,000 4/17 **Sch. 52a.** Forms/C/2118/14.

Army Form C. 2118.

WAR DIARY
or
INTELLIGENCE SUMMARY.
(Erase heading not required.)

Instructions regarding War Diaries and Intelligence Summaries are contained in F. S. Regs., Part II. and the Staff Manual respectively. Title pages will be prepared in manuscript.

Place	Date	Hour	Summary of Events and Information	Remarks and references to Appendices
MEULTE(?)	22nd		Conference at Bn. HQ - morning. Evening Camp at S.A.A. Dump	
			about 11.30pm Hd Front.	
	23rd		Working Parties as above.	
	24th		Working parties.	
	25th		One Company on working parties only.	
	26th		Working parties to WATOGRAVE(?)	
	27th		Move by rail & from YPRES TRIANGLE to ABEELE	
WATOU AREA	28th		TRAINING. Corps Commander inspected "E" Coy Billets.	
	29th		TRAINING.	
	30th		C.O. inspected Dinner.	
	31st		Box Training. Football match. D Coy v rest of the Bn Concert in YMCA Hut by the Ruffles (20th Royal Fusiliers Concert party).	

R Beckett Capt.
for Major.
Comdg. The Battalion.

1/1/18

WAR DIARY of 1st Battalion, the Lancashire Fusiliers (Scottish Rifles).

(Erase heading not required.)

Place	Date	Hour	Summary of Events and Information	Remarks and references to Appendices
WATOU	JAN. 1st		In the morning a football match was played between D Coy and the Rest of the Battalion. D Coy winning. The game was watched by the Divisional General. The men had their New Years dinner at 1.30, which the Commanding Officer went round inspecting.	
	2nd	9.30	Training. Two companies on Range. Remainder on Drill Bayonet Fighting & musketry Lecture in WATOU on billets.	
	3rd	9.0	Battalion paraded at 9 A.M. marched to ABEELE & entrained at 9 A.M. went via ST JUST to LAWRENCE CAMP BRANDHOEK.	
	4th		Battalion paraded at 10.40 A.M. & marched to ALNWICK CAMP ST JEAN.	
	5th	2.30	Battalion paraded at 2.30 P.M. & marched up to HAMBURG in relief of 2nd R.W.F. Relieving H.Q. at ISKOSME, the whole Battalion being in the new Battalion H.Q. There were no casualties (slight) loss after relieving up.	
	6th		Very quiet. Two conferences held at had an Creeden Ridge. The two conferences made for moving up to the two front line Battalions. The Artillery at HAALEN SUPPORT were reinforced.	

Army Form C. 2118.

WAR DIARY
or
INTELLIGENCE SUMMARY.
(Erase heading not required.)

Instructions regarding War Diaries and Intelligence Summaries are contained in F. S. Regs., Part II. and the Staff Manual respectively. Title pages will be prepared in manuscript.

Place	Date	Hour	Summary of Events and Information	Remarks and references to Appendices
LINE	Jan'y 7th		Slight Shelling at intervals during the day. Liason established between machine & battalion on right & on left. In the evening enemy	
	8th		had several rounds into HAMBURG. 2 men were killed, three wounded. Quiet all day until the evening Enemy shelled SEINE & HAMBURG.	
			K.I.A. three men, 1 wounding in flame.	
			Battalion relieved by 9th H.L.I & marched back to WAITRY CAMP & A.R. by 9 P.M.	
BRANDHOEK	9th		Battalion entrained in camp a light Railway & moved back to TORONTO CAMP BRANDHOEK. Transport by road	
	10th		Cleaning up, Inspections, Baths.	
	11th		Commanding Officer inspected Companies & Camp. Lectures in both Gas & Baths.	
	12th		All Companies inspected in handling Stree by the Commanding Officer. Kit Inspections. General Plumer visited the Battalion in the afternoon. Commanding Officer on leave.	
SUPPORT LINE SEINE			Battalion paraded at 7.15 A.M. Entrained at BRANDHOEK and taken up	

WAR DIARY or INTELLIGENCE SUMMARY.

Army Form C. 2118.

Place	Date	Hour	Summary of Events and Information	Remarks and references to Appendices
			to SEAHAM CAMP. The Battalion had dinners & Teas there and fell in again at 4.30 P.M. Guides met Companions at FROST HOUSE at 5.15 P.M. and went up to SEINE by JUDAH TRACK in relief of the 2nd A.S.H.R. Relief complete at 7 P.M. Very quiet night. Frost during night.	
SEINE	14th		Working parties. 2 Officers & 100 O.R. at 6.15 A.M. carrying for 171 Tunnelling Coy to CREST FARM. 2 Officers & 60 O.R. wiring BELLEVUE SWITCH under 222 Bde at 7 A.M. All Companies had pushed out wiring the posts which are to be held in case of attack.	
			No shelling near SEINE. Enemy aircraft flew low over SEINE & HAMBURG during the night. Enemy status round SEINE with 4.2's.	
	15th		Towards during night, ground very heavy. Some of the men shelters fell in, which was indian very uncomfortable. Carrying and wiring parties as for 14th. Rained heavily during the afternoon & night. Some shelling wiring the night with 4.2's.	
	16th		Usual carrying and wiring parties. Quiet during morning. Some shelling	

WAR DIARY or INTELLIGENCE SUMMARY.

Army Form C. 2118.

Place	Date	Hour	Summary of Events and Information	Remarks and references to Appendices
SEINE	17th		Of whole Trench lined of SEINE DUMP. Frost again during night. Carrying Dummy bodies to ward. Battalion faced at 5 pm.	
LINE.		6.9.	6. g. to the line in relief of the 2nd A & S.H. in the Lys Sector PASSCHENAELE. Very quiet relief which was complete at about 8:30 P.M. Two Companies (A & B) in the line. D in Support at CREST FARM & C in Reserve at HAALEN SWITCH. Bn Q. INDIGO.	
	18th		Fairly quiet all day. Some shelling in PASSCHENDAELE at intervals. Bursts of m.g. fire along main PASSCHENDAELE ROAD at night. Strong wind all day which dried up the surface of the ground a little.	
	19th		Considerable shelling much aerial activity. Battalion relieved by 16th K.R.C. completed by 8.30 P.M. Marches to light Railway near FROSTHOUSE & entrained for BRANDHOEK. Last Company arrived in camp at mid-night.	
TO CAMP	20		Cleaning up and Baths.	
BRANDHOEK	21st		Inspection of Clothing etc.	

Army Form C. 2118.

WAR DIARY
or
INTELLIGENCE SUMMARY.
(Erase heading not required.)

Instructions regarding War Diaries and Intelligence Summaries are contained in F. S. Regs., Part II. and the Staff Manual respectively. Title pages will be prepared in manuscript.

Place	Date	Hour	Summary of Events and Information	Remarks and references to Appendices
TORONTO CAMP	22nd		Inspection. Full Kit ditting prior to going into the line. Transportation Officer Paraded for Inspection by Commanding Officer.	
	23rd	2.45 P.M.	Battalion paraded at 2.45 P.M. Entrained at BRANDHOEK and taken up by lt to LOW FARM. Guides of 1st MIDDLESEX met companies at junction of JUDAH & K Tracks at 5.15 P.M. and taken in to left sector. C & D Coys in line A in Support at CREST FARM. B in Reserve at HAALEN SWITCH. Bn H Q at INDIGO HSE. Quiet relief. Some machine gun fire during the night from MOORSLEDE & WESTROOSBEKE.	
	24th		Some shelling of parts of Regt. frontage & in PASSCHENDAELE. Our Artillery active. Quiet during night except some hostile gun activity.	
	25th		Quiet day. Battalion relieved by 1/6 K.R.R. & went back to BRANDHOEK by train from LOW FARM.	
	26th		Cleaning up. Inspection. Baths. Transport parties at 8 A.M. and went by ? to OUDEZEELE.	

WAR DIARY
or
INTELLIGENCE SUMMARY.
(Erase heading not required.)

Army Form C. 2118.

Place	Date	Hour	Summary of Events and Information	Remarks and references to Appendices
BRANDHOEK	Feb 27		Battalion moved at 12.45 p.m. marched to BRANDHOEK Station, entrained for STOMER, handed over to STOMER to ST MARTIN on LAERT arriving at 7 p.m.	
	28		Cleaning up and inspections	
	29		Company Drill. Inspections.	
	30		Musketry. Company Drill. S.B. Refresher Drill & Bayonet Fighting. Regtl officers marched for the Brigadier General in Command. Officer installed. 4 hours other morning work. Equivalent Training order.	
	31st		11 a details in marching order. Company Drill. Miniature Range. I.R.R. Drill. Bomb Throwing. All companies hinted for inspection by Commanding Officer in bulking out dress.	

C. Scott
Major
the Cameronians
Commanding

Secret

WAR DIARY of 1st Battalion the Cameronians (Scottish Rifles)
INTELLIGENCE SUMMARY

Army Form C. 2118.

(Erase heading not required.)

Vol A 3

Instructions regarding War Diaries and Intelligence Summaries are contained in F. S. Regs., Part II. and the Staff Manual respectively. Title pages will be prepared in manuscript.

Place	Date	Hour	Summary of Events and Information	Remarks and references to Appendices
ST MARTIN AU LEART	1918 Sept 1st	9-12.30	A and B coys on the Range C coy making 2 Practices at 200x Snap shooting with iron foresight (5 rounds) Deliberate with hood sight (5 rounds) Ore Practice at 300 yards deliberate (5 rounds) D coy Specialist Training	89.11 10 whole
		10pm	C and D coys on Range B coy marching Same Practices as above.	
			Companies marched out to the Range in marching order.	
	2nd	7AM	Officers Riding School	
		9-10	Company Drill and Handling Arms	
		10-12.30	Specialist Training. Draft of 680 O.R. arrived	
		2 Pm	Football League. Transport v Battalion HQ.	
	3rd		Church Parade. Inspection of draft. Nearly all men from 4th Battalion and had not been out before	
	4th 9AM		C and D coys on the Range. A coy marking. 1 Practice at 205x Snap shooting (5 rounds) iron sight. 2 Practice at 300x Ore deliberate (5 rounds). A coy to do same rapid 5 rounds iron sight. B coy Specialist Training. A & D coys had dinner on Range	
		1PM	A & B coys firing practices as above. D coy marking	

WAR DIARY
or
INTELLIGENCE SUMMARY.

(Erase heading not required.)

Army Form C. 2118.

Instructions regarding War Diaries and Intelligence Summaries are contained in F. S. Regs., Part II. and the Staff Manual respectively. Title pages will be prepared in manuscript.

Place	Date	Hour	Summary of Events and Information	Remarks and references to Appendices
ST MARTIN	6th	7 A.M.	Recruits School for Officers	
LAERT		8-9	A Coy Wiring. D Coy at Musketry Range	
			B & C Coy Musketry	
		9.10	All Company Platoon and Company Drill. Draft under R.S.M.	
		11-12:30	Specialist Training	
		2-3 P.M.	Physical Training and Bayonet fighting	
		2.45	Officers & N.C.O.s under R.S.M.	
		5.30 P.M.	Lewis Gun Pack Mule Drill	
	7th	1 P.M.	Padura School	
		8-30	Companies at Baths. The remainder of the time was spent in doing Company Drill	
		-2	Battalion Bomb Drill. Artillery formation. Company Drill	
		2 P.M.	Specialist Training	
	7th	7 A.M.	Riding School	
		9-10	A Coy Miniature Range. B Coy Wiring. C & D Company Drill	
		10-11	Extended Order Drill & Artillery formation	
		11.30	Battalion Drill should have taken place but it rained	
		12.30		

WAR DIARY
or
INTELLIGENCE SUMMARY.

Army Form C. 2118.

Place	Date	Hour	Summary of Events and Information	Remarks and references to Appendices
ST MARTIN au LAERT	Feb 8th		Rained nearly the whole morning. Companies did musketry & Specialist Training in their billets turning a show for interval Physical Training & Bayonet Fighting.	
		2 P.m.	Lecture given from a hundred Ranges, Bomber, & Rifle Grenadier firing line.	
	9th	9 Am	Company Drill.	
		10 Am	2 Companies on musketry Range. Company turning & firing live R.G.grenades & smoke bombs – live bomb throwing. Company Practice on Pan Run & in the Drill- Bayonet & Physical. Lewis Gun, Bomber, & Rifle Grenadier practicing each to live.	
			Each Company practices 1 Platoon for A.R.A. Competition.	
		2.30 P.m	Football match against 2nd Scottish Rifles. Commencing at 4-0?	
	10th		Church Parade	

Army Form C. 2118.

WAR DIARY
or
INTELLIGENCE SUMMARY.
(Erase heading not required.)

Instructions regarding War Diaries and Intelligence Summaries are contained in F. S. Regs., Part II. and the Staff Manual respectively. Title pages will be prepared in manuscript.

Place	Date	Hour	Summary of Events and Information	Remarks and references to Appendices
ST MARTIN au LAERT	Feb 11	7 A.m.	Rouser Chaos	
		9-11	A Coy Company Drill - Box Respirator Drill - musketry	
			D " - musketry & Box Respirator Drill	
			Wiring -	
		11-12.30	All Conference Attack & Defence Coy & Company attacking -	
			1 selected Platoon from each company practises for A R A Competition	
		2-3	Officers & N.C.O.'s not leaves of the tyrone under the Regimental	
			Sgt Major	
	Feb 12	7AM	Rising School for Officers	
		9-11	A & B Companies on Miniature Range	
		9-10	B & C Companies Company Drill	
		10-11	musketry & Box Respirator Drill	
		11-12.30	All Companies Attack & Defence	
		2-3	Specialist Training	
			Rewolver Practice	
	Feb 13	9-10	B & C Companies on Miniature Range, Lewis Gun firing -	
			D Coy Wiring. A Company musketry, Drill Box Respirator Drill	

(A7090). Wt. W12539/M1293 757,000. 1/17. D. D. & L., Ltd. Forms/C2118/4

Army Form C. 2118.

WAR DIARY
or
INTELLIGENCE SUMMARY.
(Erase heading not required.)

Instructions regarding War Diaries and Intelligence Summaries are contained in F. S. Regs., Part II. and the Staff Manual respectively. Title pages will be prepared in manuscript.

Place	Date	Hour	Summary of Events and Information	Remarks and references to Appendices
ST MARTIN au-LAERT	Feb 13th		Rained all out of the morning. Platoon dist Training in their billets. A draft of 2 L.G.R. arrived.	
	14th		All Companies on the Range. A Coy fired 2 practices. The first 5 rounds deliberate 400x bursts fired 2 10 rounds rapid 400x. A think mist came down 2 the other companies fired 5 rounds deliberate at 200x.	
	15th		1 Platoon from each company practised for the C.R.A. Competition. All Platoons for ARA Competition practised on horse draw Range. Remainder of Coys - Company Drill - Musketry - Short Range Respirator tests in gas hut. In the afternoon the Transport were inspected by the Brigadier and afterwards by O.C. Train.	
	16th		In the morning 1 Platoon from each Company fired off the ARA Competition Drill Platoon Drill &c. In the afternoon the winning Platoon from	

WAR DIARY or INTELLIGENCE SUMMARY

Army Form C. 2118.

Place	Date	Hour	Summary of Events and Information	Remarks and references to Appendices
	17th		Route Marches in the Brigade completed & No 13 Platoon (Lt McLean) were The remainder of the companies were on the miniature Range until 11 A.M. from 11.30 - 12.30 Battalion Sick & Burial Pde. Church Parade.	
	18th	11.15	General Quincy presents Medals & Watches & afterwards addressed the battalion. The battalion marched past the G.O.C. in Column of Platoons. A demonstration was given by the H.Q. Battalion in Barrages. In the morning No 12 Platoon taken over by Lowry to the 4th Army Musketry School Range, to compete against Platoon of 78th & 10th & 15th in a R.A. Exhibition. The Platoon of the Camerons fired first & scored 300 bomb, 229 kits on the Targets, 94 discs on back pieces, 21 points above us for style. The Lovat staghorn boys of 10th Bde fired next and scored 287 bomb and last the Argyll & Sutherlands Highlanders of 98th Bde whose score 277. The Platoon were congratulated by General Pinney -	

Place	Date	Hour	Summary of Events and Information	Remarks and references to Appendices
ST MARTIN au LAERT	Feb 18		In the afternoon Brigade Revolver Competition was held for the Revolver & Individual Prize. Three Officers & 3 OR's from each Batta. competed. This was won by Lt Whitwick of the Battalion. In the Evening a lecture was given by the Divisional Gas Officer on "Respirators, Projectors". Transport left right P.M. Stopping at RENESCURE 10½°, STEENVOORDE 10½°. BRANDHOEK 20. Battalion arrived at 7.20 A.M. for practice in dropping	Aeroplane warfare & The Company interchanged
	Feb 19 -20		at low flying Aeroplanes. After breakfast 9 am Class was held over the Battalion. Battalion entrained at 6.30 A.M., marched to Hopoutre & Entrained leaving at 9 A.M. Detrained at Ypres & 11.45 A.M. went into billets in between Ypres & taking over from 8th D.L.I.	

Army Form C. 2118.

WAR DIARY
or
INTELLIGENCE SUMMARY.
(Erase heading not required.)

Instructions regarding War Diaries and Intelligence Summaries are contained in F. S. Regs., Part II. and the Staff Manual respectively. Title pages will be prepared in manuscript.

Place	Date	Hour	Summary of Events and Information	Remarks and references to Appendices
YPRES	Feb 21	4.45	In the morning 2nd Battalion prep to going into the line. A and B Coys & 2 Platoons C Coy left by train from Barrack Siding Ypres.	
PASSCHENDAELE		5.15	Remainder of C Coy & D Coy by tram. Detrained at IBERIA, marched via HTR k tracks to left sub sector in relief of 5th Yorkshire Regt 50th Division. Quiet night with the exception of some shelling near KANSDURG Dispositions A Coy. Right B Coy Left C " 2 Platoons PASSCHENDAELE Road. ½ C & D CREST FARM Battn H.Q. HAMBURG	
		2.30	Rain in morning. Little shelling all day. Wind westerly fine at night.	

WAR DIARY
or
INTELLIGENCE SUMMARY.

(Erase heading not required.)

Army Form C.

Place	Date	Hour	Summary of Events and Information	Remarks and references to Appendices
PASSCHENDAELE	Feb 23		Heavy Shelling on PASSCHENDAELE Church and track leading up to it from CREST FARM. "D" Company relief "B" relieved "A" on right. "C" hrs relieved "B". "A" & "B" Coy at CREST FARM. Relief 2Lts at 6.30 P.M. Completed by 8 P.M. At 11.45 P.M. S.O.S. Signal was sent up on the right of the Div[?] front shortly followed by S.O.S on left Div[?] front, there was S.O.S. fire at HILLSIDE. Our artillery transport came very quickly. Conference reports no sign of Enemy on their front. Enemy put down fierce barrage between CREST FARM & PASSCHENDAELE. All quiet by 12.30 A.M.	
	24th		Enemy shelled the church all day. In the evening a shed behind Ch.	

WAR DIARY
or
INTELLIGENCE SUMMARY.
(Erase heading not required.)

Army Form C. 2118.

Place	Date	Hour	Summary of Events and Information	Remarks and references to Appendices
Whitley Camp	Feb 25th		Snipers Coken where support platoon & left company were training. Some of the men. One man was hit by D.E. wounded.	
	26th		Quiet during day. Battalion was relieved by 1st Middlesex Regiment. Having sent own several bursts of fire & there were 4 casualties in B Coy. line back to Whitley Camp.	
	27th		Inspection & cleaning up.	
			Baths. Lecture on shell hole defences. Inter Coy Rapid L.G. Drill.	
	28th	6:45 AM	Whole Battalion out a working Parties under R.E. in Army Line at LOW FARM. UHLAN FARM.	

C.P. Scott
Major
Commanding The Camerons.

WAR DIARY of 1st Bn. the Cameronians (Scottish Rifles)

Army Form C. 2118

Place	Date	Hour	Summary of Events and Information	Remarks and references to Appendices
PASSCHENDAELE	March 1st		The Battalion marches up to the line in relief of 1st MIDDLESEX REGT (98th Bde); left WHITBY CAMP 1.30 PM using H.O.K. – JUDAH & MULE Tracks. Battalion in support to the 13th Battalion HQ at IRKSOME. Provides carrying parties for the other 2 Battalions. Quiet day with occasional shelling.	
"	2nd		Quiet during the day. A lad was carried out by the Division on our left during which the S.O.S. was sent up from somewhere believed on left.	unknown
"	3rd		Bn. H.Q. Our barrage came down quickly & there was a good deal of retaliation by the enemy. Another S.O.S. was sent up about 2 hours later further to the north.	
"	4th		Enemy had two or three areo shoots which lasted about 10 minutes each, mostly 4.2". McConnell killed.	
"	5th		Battalion relieved by 1st MIDDLESEX at about 4.30 P.M. March back to Divisional Reserve. WHITBY CAMP.	
WHITBY CAMP.	6th		The whole battalion out working on the ARMY Defence Line from 9 – 2 PM	

T.O. 11
13 Mar.

WAR DIARY
or
INTELLIGENCE SUMMARY.
(Erase heading not required.)

Army Form C. 2118.

Instructions regarding War Diaries and Intelligence Summaries are contained in F. S. Regs., Part II. and the Staff Manual respectively. Title pages will be prepared in manuscript.

Place	Date	Hour	Summary of Events and Information	Remarks and references to Appendices
WHITBY CAMP	Mond 7th		Working party 4. Officers 150 O.R. working for R.E.	
	8th		Bathing and Trench Foot Treatment. Officer sent up to reconnoitre right sub-sector of the left Brigate.	
LINE	9th		The Battalion relieves 2nd Argyll & Sutherland Hrs in right sub sector known from DECOYWOOD on the right to PARK CHENDAELE DETECT CROSSING Road on the left. The Queen's on the left of the Battalion & Glasgow Highlanders on the right— Left WHITBY CAMP by train at 5.20 P.M. detrained LOW FARM, from there by JUDAH TRACK. Guides met Battn at HAMBURG — A Coy LEFT FRONT Coy B " RIGHT " " C " SUPPORT HAALEN SWITCH D " " HILLSIDE & KEERSELAARHOEK	

WAR DIARY
or
INTELLIGENCE SUMMARY.
(Erase heading not required.)

Army Form C. 2118.

Place	Date	Hour	Summary of Events and Information	Remarks and references to Appendices
LINE	March 9th		Battalion H.Q. INDIGO. Quiet Relief- from afft. Balty was complete being Shelling in retaliation for our harassing fire.	
	10th		Above shelled by enemy throughout the day in reply to our fire.	
	11th		At 2 AM SOS went up on the front of the Division on our left. Heavy attacks to about 20 minutes. At 3 A.m another heavy burst of fire from enemy & again at 5 A.m until about 5.20. Lt Col. Stokes, who was temporarily commanding the Brigade was hit here HAALEN SWITCH	
	12th		Fairly quiet all day- later Lay relieved D achievis A Coy and C relieves B. Quiet night	
	13th		Quiet all day and also during the night with the exception of some trench mortar fire. Lt Col Shea acting Brigadier was wounded by	

WAR DIARY
or
INTELLIGENCE SUMMARY.

Army Form C. 2118.

Place	Date	Hour	Summary of Events and Information	Remarks and references to Appendices
LINE	14		Fine weather. Quiet day. At 11 P.m. a chernite came over from the enemy lines and informed Brigade that a raid was to take place at 1 A.m. between the ZONNEBEKE Rly & GRAVENSTAFEL was (GRN Pat) GRUN Pat. This was actually to take place, but the enemy party was caught by our batteries which opened up at 12.55 A.m. The enemy was also caught by our Lewis gun fire & severed [severed?] the enemy were killed & the remainder taken. 2 tm also strength of raid about 60 men.	
"	15		Battalion in reserve by 1st Border Regt in light curl-Bullets returned at LOW FARM & the truck to MAIDEN CAMP.	
MAIDEN CAMP	16		Cleaning up and Baths. Sgt Cocker was awarded Meritorious Service Medal for 3 v wy Service now [?]	

Army Form C. 2118.

WAR DIARY
or
INTELLIGENCE SUMMARY.
(Erase heading not required)

Instructions regarding War Diaries and Intelligence Summaries are contained in F. S. Regs., Part II. and the Staff Manual respectively. Title pages will be prepared in manuscript.

Place	Date	Hour	Summary of Events and Information	Remarks and references to Appendices
MAIDEN CAMP	17th		From a bad accident, 2nd Lt Thorney a new Patten bomb a new lot on Drill after the supply for his had been taken out. Sgt Locher 2nd in and pulled the bomb up & threw it clear, the undoubtedly saved several men from serious wounds. Church Parade.	
	18th		2 Companies working on Army Defence Zone in the morning. Running companies on work in Camp. The Camp was shelled during the afternoon by a 15" gun. One shell fell very near a tent killing 2 men Volunteers [?]. and wounding 16 others.	
	19th		The Brigade moved back to RRANDHOEK in consequence of the Shelling. The Battalion left MAIDEN CAMP at 11 A.M. and marched to TORONTO CAMP.	
	20th		Battalion working on Army Zone Defences – Private 2 A.M. & went	

WAR DIARY
or
INTELLIGENCE SUMMARY.
(Erase heading not required.)

Army Form C. 2118.

Place	Date	Hour	Summary of Events and Information	Remarks and references to Appendices
BRANDHOEK	20th		by Light Railway to BORRY FARM, relieving about 1 P.m. Raising party of 30 men from A Company paraded at 4 A.m and went up to CREST FARM for the day. Battalion paraded 5 P.m. for the line. By Light Railway to	

LINE	21st		BORRY FARM from BRANDHOEK, thence by JUDAH TRACK. Relieved 2nd Argyles Putteries Highlanders in left sub. sector Division. C Company - Left Front
			                D " Right "
			Hqrs 2 Platoon B. PASSCHENDAELE.ROAD.
			     W/H Q 2 " CREST FARM
			     A Company CREST FARM
			     Battalion H.Q. HAMBURG.
			Raid on GASOMETERS
			Raiding party 3 officers & 20 O.R. A Company paraded in CREST FARM dug out at 11.25 P.m. and move off by the track to the Right Company H.Q. ate 11.45 P.m.	

WAR DIARY
INTELLIGENCE SUMMARY

Army Form C. 2118.

Place	Date	Hour	Summary of Events and Information	Remarks and references to Appendices
LINE	March 21st		4/150.R The raiding party was divided into 4 groups, two under Lt GORELY, of which one was directly under him and the other under Sgt Young; and two under Lt LIESK, of which one was directly under him and the other under Cpl Lockie. (150.R) The covering party under Lt BROWN was divided into 3 parties, two of which formed twin Gun Teams of 4 men under Cpl Saunders & Cpl Bennet respectively, the third a group of riflemen under Sgt Pyke. Two Stretcher bearers accompanied Sgt Pyke. A bugler accompanies the party. Almost immediately after leaving the dug out, a shell burst in the track which knocks out the whole of Lt Gorelys party killing 1 man & wounding 6 others. Rt. Gp. Company H.Q. was reached at 12:5 A.M. Here men to make up Lt Gottles party has previously by D Coy & the parties returned.	

WAR DIARY
or
INTELLIGENCE SUMMARY

Army Form C. 2118.

Place	Date	Hour	Summary of Events and Information	Remarks and references to Appendices
LINE	March 22nd		As soon as the reorganisation was completed the patrol proceeded out to No 8 Post, which was reached at 12.30 A.M. Previously it had been decided to send out a tape $150°$ to the Gasometers, but owing to the brightness of the moon this was only put out 50° as a guide towards the objective, also to serve as a guide through a gap in our wire. Owing to the bright moon crawling was resorted to from No 8 Post which was the proper plan. No incident occurred during the forward crawl and the position was presently formed up about $100°$ from the GASOMETERS at 1.47 A.M. The patrol formed up as follows: from left to right — Lt Cole, Sgt Young, Cpl Welsh, Lt Liddle. These were at intervals of $20°$ between parties. Cpl Kennedy, Sgt Tyler, Cpl Lawson. Lt Peden was with the centre party. The Artillery & T.M. Barrage came down promptly at 2.5 A.M. but	

WAR DIARY
or
INTELLIGENCE SUMMARY.

Army Form C. 2118.

Place	Date	Hour	Summary of Events and Information	Remarks and references to Appendices
LINE	March 2nd		The M.G. teams of Nos 30 & 19 left behind. The raiding parties have returned in perfect order but everwhere no opposition. About 40x from the objective 2 belts of wire were found, & these would have formed a serious obstacle if there had been any opposition. The G. amatisse were examined but found to contain no trace of habitation, & there was no s/g. of anything dug out. There was however, a shell hole post outside the above mentioned wire which looks to have been inhabited recently. Beyond this there was no s/g. of the enemy occupying this area at all. The enemy meanwhile has not fired a rifle that A.M.G. has known to have fired on the left apparently up the MOORSLEDE road, this was taken on by the Lewis gun of the covering party & did not fire	

WAR DIARY
or
INTELLIGENCE SUMMARY.

(Erase heading not required.)

Army Form C. 2118.

Place	Date	Hour	Summary of Events and Information	Remarks and references to Appendices
LINE	March 2nd		Again. The raising party remained at 6 hours round the farm line and proved back again through the covering party at 2.17 A.m. but on the high (the bigged to white) was Chown. The covering party remained at 5 hours longer & were back at No. 8 Post by 2.30 A.M. A red Very light was sent up from R? Company H.Q. as a signal for the returning party, which proved late in my opinion. The whole party then returned to ELFIT FARM. The remainder of the day was quiet in front but from 4 A.M – 8 A.M the enemy shelled our trestern position in the farm at the rate of 50 to shells a minute.	

WAR DIARY
or
INTELLIGENCE SUMMARY.

(Erase heading not required.)

Army Form C. 2118.

Place	Date	Hour	Summary of Events and Information	Remarks and references to Appendices
LINE	March 23rd		Quiet during the day and night.	
	24th		Quiet. Company Relief. A Company relieved D	
			B " " A	
			C " " B	
	25th		Lt. Col. J.H.C. Drysdale D.S.O. took over command of the Battalion. During the afternoon he was very heavily shelling for 3/4 hr. Chiefly on the PASSCHENDAELE Road. A Stretcher bearer killed & 1 other wounded of C Coy.	
	26th		At 11 P.m. an Battle Patrol of 1 Officer & 12 O.R went out from the 9 o'meter. A Patrol of the enemy about 25 strong were to be seen. On patrol was seen by the enemy. At that moment the enemy barrage came down and almost at once our own February. The enemy then withdrew & our patrol having finished its task were ordered by the O.C. to return & on S.O.S front was sent up by the Divison.	

WAR DIARY
or
INTELLIGENCE SUMMARY.
(Erase heading not required.)

Army Form C. 2118.

Place	Date	Hour	Summary of Events and Information	Remarks and references to Appendices
			on our left and the enemy tried to crawl through which proved to be a failure.	
	27th	3:45 P.M.	A party of the enemy was seen from one of the posts & on left company to be approaching our own line that were first sent. Then & the enemy disappeared. Five minutes later the enemy put down a T.M. Barrage, which remained for 2 minutes, then lifted. Two parties were then seen to be approaching on foot one from the front & the other on the left flank. Bomb's with him were opened on them & they were driven off – The Battalion was relieved by 1st Mx Middlesex Regt and returned	
BRANDHOEK 28th			by Light Railway to BRANDHOEK. Ins Luttrain's Clearing up.	

Army Form C. 2118.

WAR DIARY
or
INTELLIGENCE SUMMARY.
(Erase heading not required.)

Instructions regarding War Diaries and Intelligence Summaries are contained in F. S. Regs., Part II. and the Staff Manual respectively. Title pages will be prepared in manuscript.

Place	Date	Hour	Summary of Events and Information	Remarks and references to Appendices
BRANDHOEK	29th		Coys & Companies working on Divisional Line. C Coy had 2 men casualties. At 12 noon Ltkw. Lt Clay wounded. 4 men Ot.Rs & 6 wounded OR. Show two companies training.	
	30th		The whole battalion working on Divisional Line. Parade 8 AM returned to Farm Bding, boarded IBERIA before finished 2.20 PM. Returned by tea from IBERIA.	
	31st		2 Coys working on Army Defence Line. At 1 PM Parade moved to be ready to move at 1 hour notice. At 3 PM orders received to proceed by bus to an unknown destination. Parade 4.15 PM left BRANDHOEK by bus at 9 PM. Detrained between near HÉNENCOURT about 12 mls to East of ALBERT.	

19th Brigade.
33rd Division.

1st BATTALION

CAMERONIANS (Scottish Rifles)

APRIL 1918.

… WAR DIARY of 1st Bn. "The Cameronians" (Scottish Rifles)

INTELLIGENCE SUMMARY.
(Erase heading not required.)

Place	Date	Hour	Summary of Events and Information	Remarks and references to Appendices
GRAND RULLECOURT	April 1		The Brigade moved by bus to LIENCOURT which was reached at 6.15 am. It was now in the 3rd Army being an Army Reserve. Less orders to bold itself in readiness to move at short notice. After detraining at LIENCOURT the Battalion marched about 1½ miles to billets at GRAND RULLECOURT. The billets were good, but only two were pads. Château at South end of village provided accommodation for five officers who could not get billets in the village. C.O. exception of a rifle inspection at 5:30 pm no parades were held during the day.	
	2		Parades - 9 am to 12 noon - Drawing	
	3		Parades - 9.15 am to 10 am - Battalion 10 am to 12 noon - Drawing 4.1.30 pm numbers officers attended a lecture scheme under Brig-adr arrangements.	

Army Form C. 2118.

WAR DIARY
or
INTELLIGENCE SUMMARY.
(Erase heading not required)

Instructions regarding War Diaries and Intelligence Summaries are contained in F. S. Regs., Part II. and the Staff Manual respectively. Title pages will be prepared in manuscript.

Place	Date	Hour	Summary of Events and Information	Remarks and references to Appendices
GRAND RULLECOURT	4	9.15 am 10 am to 12.15 pm	Parades 9.15 am – Battalion Parade 10 am to 12.15 pm Training. The Brigadier inspected the Battalion at work during the forenoon. At 2.15 pm the Commanding Officer lectured to all officers & NCO's on points affecting the work & discipline of the Battalion & on the general situation. During the afternoon football matches were played between D Coy (19 one) & A Coy (nil) & between B Coy (29 odd) & C Coy (nil)	
GRAND RULLECOURT	5		During the early morning the Battalion was prepared to move forward at short notice. At noon in accordance with orders the Batt.n left GRAND RULLECOURT and marched via WESNES-LES-COMPTE – HERBECQ to "Y" Camp on the main ST POL – ARRAS Road about ½ mile N of DUISANS. This camp was reached at 4.30 pm & accommodates the whole Brigade.	
Y Camp	6	10 am – 12.30 pm	Parades 10 am – 12.30 pm Training. During the afternoon Lewis gun sections fired on the miniature range	

WAR DIARY
or
INTELLIGENCE SUMMARY.
(Erase heading not required.)

Army Form C. 2118.

Place	Date	Hour	Summary of Events and Information	Remarks and references to Appendices
Y Camp	7		The Batt. received orders to move back to GRANDE RULLECOURT next morning.	
			The Batt. left Y Camp at 7.40 a.m. & marched by same mule track to GRANDE RULLECOURT which was reached at 12.15 p.m. The Brigadier Gunner complimenting the Batn on its smart turnout & marching.	
			The views of both new officers were not so good as in the previous season because the whole division had now assembled in the area. The 19th Field Ambulance, 11th Trench Coy RE were also sheltered in the village.	
			At 9.30 p.m. 5 Officers 152 OR who had been allotted as BRAND HOEK after the Brigade 2/C. returned to the Base. Duty consisted of men from leave or the regimental empty and a draft of 27 men who had come by train to AUBIGNY thence marched to GRANDE RULLECOURT	
GRANDE RULLECOURT	8		The Divnan moa in BHQ reserve. Morning Parades 8.45 a.m. — 12.45 p.m. — Range & Drawing at LIENCOURT at 3 p.m. the Divisional General Review Battalion Drill.	

Army Form C. 2118.

WAR DIARY
or
INTELLIGENCE SUMMARY.
(Erase heading not required.)

Instructions regarding War Diaries and Intelligence Summaries are contained in F. S. Regs., Part II. and the Staff Manual respectively. Title pages will be prepared in manuscript.

Place	Date	Hour	Summary of Events and Information	Remarks and references to Appendices
GRANDE RULLECOURT	9		Officers & NCOs of the Brigade were lectured in the evening on the recent fighting. At 6 pm a regimental crest was held.	
"	10		Training was carried out during the morning and afternoon. Two officers & battalion started at B.H.Q at 8 AM to go and reconnoitre the green line near ADINFER and BLAIREVILLE this was held by a Brigade of Guards' Division. About noon the Batt= received orders to hold itself ready to move at one hours notice. Orders were received at 3-30PM to be ready to move at once. At 9 pm the Batt= marched to AUBIGNY.	
"	11		AUBIGNY was reached at 1-30 AM. after waiting for four hours the Batt= entrained & reached CAESTRE at 3-15 PM. Here extra ammunition was issued, and the Batt= marched to a field on the western outskirts of METEREN	

WAR DIARY
or
INTELLIGENCE SUMMARY.
(Erase heading not required.)

Army Form C. 2118.

Place	Date	Hour	Summary of Events and Information	Remarks and references to Appendices
	11		and bivouacked for the night. The Brigade was in Corps Reserve. Lt A.G. ROBB M.C. joined the Batt's line. "C" Company sent a platoon on outpost duty to guard approaches from the SOUTH.	
METEREN	12	11 AM	Patrols were sent out into MERRIS and STRAZEELE and discovered that these places were held by us, the former very lightly and by details of their own division. A patrol under Lt A.G. ROBB M.C. reached the outskirts of the village of OULTERSTEENE which was in enemy hands. At 11 AM "B" Coy was sent to support the Queens	
		1:30PM	The rest of the Batt's less the minimum reserve moved to X.13.d.0.9. along with a company of the 2nd N.Z. Entrenching B? which had been attached. A gap had been made in the line between X.25.c.7.5 and X.26.B.2.4. from this latter point Eastwards the line was held by the Queens the Batt's was ordered to fill up the gap. "C" Coy were ordered to do this. A personal reconnaissance was made by the Commanding Officer who has been taking Charge of the whole forward area from	

Place	Date	Hour	Summary of Events and Information	Remarks and references to Appendices
	12		STRAZEELE (inclusive) to the right flank of the Queens at X26.b.2.4. It was discovered that the line from X25.c.15 westwards to STRAZEELE was held by the 9/2D Bde. Reinforcements and remnants of 31st & 34th Divisions hit the 4th Australians in support. This part of the line was taken up by the Australians on the night of 13th/14th. Between X25.b.15 and X25.c.7.8. the line was held by remnants of 31st 34th & 50th Divisions all of whom had been fighting for several days and never seem to have been considered available and D'ion were ordered to take up a position at X25.a. in support to them, and to fill up any gap. BHQ of 4th Australians now at STRAZEELE and during the afternoon liaison between them was maintained by each having a cyclist orderly at each the HQn was found to be of the utmost importance when orders were received that the 33rd Divisional was about to retire and join up with the Australians at X19.c.29. The only information they had of our intention to retire was through this liaison orderly. Again we received from them a copy of the new honour line of the artillery supporting them	

WAR DIARY
or
INTELLIGENCE SUMMARY.
(Erase heading not required.)

Army Form C. 2118.

Place	Date	Hour	Summary of Events and Information	Remarks and references to Appendices
			This was found to cross our line and at places fell behind our supports. As the Australians had a map showing our dispositions they got into communication with their Brigade while we got into communication with our Bns. The damage being altered.	
			On account of the extent of front held by "C" Coy "A" Coy was ordered to take over half of it so that the line could be held in depth. The disposition of the Coys was now as follows. D Coy Coy 7 posts dug in X:15.a. in support "C" Coy 3 platoons in front line from X:15.a.07.5. to X:25.d.7.9 with one platoon in support about X:16.b.2.4 and one in support. The line was held by section posts about 200x in rear. Two platoons of "B" Coy were sent up to reinforce the Brisons the other two remaining in posts in reserve. The minimum reserve which had been left near METEREN rejoined the Battn. and was used to carry up ammunition to front line	

Place	Date	Hour	Summary of Events and Information	Remarks and references to Appendices
	13		The night and early forenoon passed fairly quietly. The enemy were seen in small groups at distances of 600 to 800 yds away. There made attempts to advance all along our front but were stopped by rifle and Lewis gun fire. The details holding the line from X.15.e.11. to X.15.e.75. gave way and a platoon of "D" Coy was immediately pushed up and took over the stretch of line vacated when the Australians took over the 9th Bde. Reinforcements. They held a line which had been dug in support on the undulating ground that the 19th Bde were to attack and form up with them at X.19.e.29 and three continue the line north wards the line held by the Battalion was very well sighted having a good field of fire and command of the ground to MERRIS which had been in the enemy hands since the night of the 12th. "D" Coy therefore formed up with the Australians at X.15.a.22 and to fill up the gap between this point and the right flank of the forward platoon of "D" Coy at X.25.c.15. two posts were established. About midday a determined attack developed from our left. The Queens were driven in and a gap was made between them and our "A" Coy. Our posts drew off the enemy who attacked them from the front and even when the enemy began coming through the gap and attacking from a flank	

WAR DIARY
or
INTELLIGENCE SUMMARY.

the huts of "A" Coy stood firm and those on the flank come back to support huts only when practically surrounded. In one case a hut remained firing until the enemy had closed round it and those of the garrison who survived had to lie out and crawl back but the enemy after dark. Two platoons of the N.Z. Coy were sent up to reinforce the left flank and fill the gap between "A" Coy and the Queens. This was done in a most capable manner by these men at dusk, the forward huts of "A" Coy and a few of the left huts of "C" Coy where slightly withdrawn to conform with the line held by the Queens. The two N.Z. platoons took over the front line huts and "A" Coy took up a position in support of them. Three of the four remaining officers of "A" Coy were slightly wounded during the day and Lieutenant Col. D.Coy was killed by a shell during the afternoon and was reserve from Brigade that the enemy had broken through and that enemy cavalry had been seen. The reserve at BHQ consisting of 2 platoons of the N.Z. Coy and the minimum reserve lined the road running E and W in X13 B and X14 a. BHQ moved from X13 B O.5 to X13 b.6.3 where the front companies.

(A7992). Wt. W12889/M1293 750,000. 1/17. D. D. & L., Ltd. Forms/C.2118/14.

WAR DIARY
INTELLIGENCE SUMMARY

Army Form C. 2118.

Place	Date	Hour	Summary of Events and Information	Remarks and references to Appendices
	13		afected everything meanwhile on their front there outposts were intelligence to H.Q. The platoon of B Coy in the line with the Queens neyethes there were very well hit in trees bank along with them on their flank. Sufficient gunner and ravies were both found to be missing believed killed. The following messages were received. "The Div Commander has just rung me up to say that both Corps, Army and G.H.Q are very pleased with the work done by the 19th Bn Grunt the congratulate all ranks on having earned such high praise and feel sure that all ranks will combine to stick it out. (Sgd) C Maynard Bry Gen Comdy 19th Inf Bde. 13.4.18. Three prisoners were taken by "C" Coy during the night the first time who had been slightly wounded said they had been in the line six days without being able to attack any day an attack was to have taken place that morning but was postponed on account of heavy casualties inflicted by artillery while they were preparing to attack their coy which had come into action 170 strong was reduced to 40.	

(A7093) Wt. W12819/M1693 75,000 1/17 D.D. & L., Ltd. Form/C.2118/14.

WAR DIARY
or
INTELLIGENCE SUMMARY.

Army Form C. 2118.

Place	Date	Hour	Summary of Events and Information	Remarks and references to Appendices
	14		During the morning enemy was reported massing in front of the battalion but they were greatly interfered with by our men and no serious attack developed. About 2 P.M. enemy made an attempt to pierce our line, which was repeatedly repulsed by rifle and M.G. fire. Our left flank was again enforced for a short time but our posts stood firm and the matter was soon put right by the Queens. BHQ was heavily shelled and received a direct hit R.S.M. Vinden was slightly wounded and his place taken by C.S.M. Edwards. C Coy BHQ moved back to X 13. d.5.8. As matters had quietened considerably the minimum reserve were sent back to the transport lines. "B" Coy who had been relieved with the Queens came to BHQ with suffox.	
	15		A quiet day was spent, enemy patrols were reported to have been seen on the main road between BAILLEUL and METEREN. Relieved by 5th S.R. a very bad relief.	
	16		On Relief companies marched back to FONTANE HOUEK, BHQ	

WAR DIARY
or
INTELLIGENCE SUMMARY.
(Erase heading not required.)

Army Form C. 2118.

Place	Date	Hour	Summary of Events and Information	Remarks and references to Appendices
	16		arriving there about 3 a.m. B Coy manned a trench at x 4 e, the other companies were in farms, each had a patrol guarding the roads leading to METEREN. At 6 a.m. the enemy were reported in METEREN and the Batt. was ordered to stand to. Immediately afterwards came the order to man the Red Line — a rear trench from x 9 central to x 11 a 7 6. companies took up positions in the order left to right A.C.B.D. At 1 PM a company of French infantry of the 133 Div took over part of A Coy front from x 9 central to La BEQUE 7 ME at x 9 a 17 At 8-30 PM an attack was made by the 7 inch on METEREN. They advanced in single file in two lines through the Batt's very heavy barrage was put down but the 7 inch suffered very few casualties in going through it. After dark it quite ME "A" Coy took out a patrol to see if the 7 inch had taken METEREN. On reaching the outskirts he was fired on by the enemy from one of the houses he had succeeded in	

WAR DIARY
or
INTELLIGENCE SUMMARY.

Army Form C. 2118.

Place	Date	Hour	Summary of Events and Information	Remarks and references to Appendices
	16		passing through our front line without being challenged. At 11 P.M. the Battⁿ was ordered to evacuate the trees line and proceed to R.20.c. Casualties during the day 1 officer and five men wounded.	
	17		Battⁿ was in a small cottage at R.20.c.7.6. "C" Coy officers and own men billeted in a farm near at hand, the men of the remaining Coys spent the night on the road side. During the day accommodation was found for all the men in farm and cottages but on account of shelling the whole Battⁿ moved about 300 yds to the north at dusk when the shelling ceased. The Bⁿ returned to the billets. Casualties during the day 1 killed 6 wounded.	at MONT DES CATS
	18		Battalion was ordered to prepare to relieve the the 34th Div but then later cancelled Orders were received that the Bⁿ	

WAR DIARY
or
INTELLIGENCE SUMMARY.
(Erase heading not required.)

Army Form C. 2118.

Instructions regarding War Diaries and Intelligence Summaries are contained in F. S. Regs., Part II. and the Staff Manual respectively. Title pages will be prepared in manuscript.

Place	Date	Hour	Summary of Events and Information	Remarks and references to Appendices
	18		Had to move early next morning to R 29 b. to assist the 49th Div if an expected attack by the enemy took place. Route overdue BERTHEN – been seen extra	
	19		Battalion left R 20 e. at 4-30 am arrived at La LEVRETTE R 29 b. at 5-30 am Several fields on the reverse & left of the hill were alloted to the Battn? the men dug shelter to themselves. An attack took place during the day General Chaplin D.S.O. G.O.C. 103rd Bde wanted the B.? Adrs were assured that the battalion would relieve the 7th Duke of Wellington 147th Bde 49th Div in the front line, that night from K 12.a.11 and relieve to about 5.7.6.37 SITANS CAPEL—BAILLEUL ROAD road inclusive. The front line consisted of a continuous front line trench with an immediate support of a few posts close at hand. There had been very heavy shelling and men were dug	

WAR DIARY
or
INTELLIGENCE SUMMARY.

(Erase heading not required.)

Army Form C. 2118.

Place	Date	Hour	Summary of Events and Information	Remarks and references to Appendices
	19		B and D Companies were in the front line A and C in Suffolk B + C in a cellar in the Convent of ST ANS CAPEL.	
	20		4 French officers of the 231 9 R. looked over the line during the early morning with a view to relief by them that night. The day was fairly quiet except for bursts of shelling on Roads & ST ANS CAPEL.	
	21		At 1-30 AM the Battn was relieved by a coy of the 231st French Infantry Regiment the Battalion moved back to KRUYSTRAETE R 23 d. near headquarters were served. Here the Batt⁼ met the transport and at 7 am the B⁻ de marched to aerodrome at P 25 C 7.4 south of ST MARIE CAPPEL. Total casualties during the battle 1 officer killed 1 wounded and one missing and seven wounded. 40 OR's killed 5 wounded and missing 127 missing. 125 wounded.	
	22		Infantry Brigade at training in the morning. Close order drill	

Army Form C. 2118.

WAR DIARY
or
INTELLIGENCE SUMMARY.
(Erase heading not required.)

Instructions regarding War Diaries and Intelligence Summaries are contained in F. S. Regs., Part II. and the Staff Manual respectively. Title pages will be prepared in manuscript.

Place	Date	Hour	Summary of Events and Information	Remarks and references to Appendices
	22		Quakety – P.T and B.F. Box respirator drill were practiced. The following officers joined the Battalion. Lieut R.E.Mitchell 2nd Lt Gm Wallace MM 2nd Lt FK Wallace Lt T.C Clay 2nd Lt HE Mills. Lt T E Clay had returned from hospital.	
	23		Training was carried out by companies as for 22nd	
	24		G.O.C. 33rd Div inspected the battalion and expressed his appreciation of work done during the battle. The rest of the morning was devoted to training a football match was played between officers of the B.3 and officers of 5 c.h. Result 3–1 in battalion favour	
	25		Companies were allotted the range at P 8 a.0.4. in addition one hours training was done football match	

WAR DIARY
or
INTELLIGENCE SUMMARY.

Army Form C. 2118.

(Erase heading not required.)

Place	Date	Hour	Summary of Events and Information	Remarks and references to Appendices
	26		Training was carried out by companies in the morning. In the afternoon a football match was played between quartmn and "A" Coy; resulted a draw 0-0.	
	27		A battalion field day had been arranged but owing to an order to stand to this had to be cancelled. About 11-30 PM this order was cancelled and ordinary training was done by companies. In the afternoon the officers and Regimental team played against the 2nd Argyll and Sutherland Highlanders officers match 2-1 against the 6 battalion Regimental team a draw 1-1.	
	28		The battalion paraded for Church parade at 10-15 AM after which half and an hours battalion drill was done	

WAR DIARY
or
INTELLIGENCE SUMMARY.
(*Erase heading not required*)

Army Form C. 2118.

Place	Date	Hour	Summary of Events and Information	Remarks and references to Appendices
	28		In the afternoon the officers played a football match against 5th S.R. officers. result 3-0 in 5th S.R. favour.	
	29		About 4am orders were received that the Battalion would move to RACQUINGHEM and the battalion left the camp at 10-15. After proceeding for about half a mile the move was cancelled and the Battalion returned to the camp.	
	30		Battalion drill was practised during the morning. Also companies carried out training. In the afternoon a football match was played between the officers and sergeants. Result 1-0 for sgts. During the evening messed into hands of the Division.	

F W Whitfield Lieut Colonel
Comdandng 1/7th The Somerset L.I.

WAR DIARY

INTELLIGENCE SUMMARY

1st Bn. The Cameronians (Scottish Rifles)

Place	Date	Hour	Summary of Events and Information	Remarks and references to Appendices
St MARIE CAPPELLE	May 1st		The Bn marched from Arnoisons near St Marie CAPELLE to RACQUINGHAM where tents & a field were provided for accommodation of Battalion. Dinners were eaten on the line of march at EBBLINGHEM. The following Officers joined the Bn. Lt J.B. Anderson, Lt J. McLeella 7th J.4 Res. Bn.; 2/Lt A.W.R. Steel; 2/Lt D. Thorjean; 2/Lt D. Eades 9/11; 2/Lt J. Drynan 9/11; 2/Lt A. Brodie	
RACQUINGHAM	2nd		Battalion Parade for Bn. Drill & Bracketing Artillery formation on fours. Guns near Gillets - Corps Fire on Range - Practices carried out s'annuts deliberate, 5 rounds rapid. Specialist classes carried out under Bn Corps instructors. Instructors.	
	2nd		The Bn entrained at RACQUINGHEM for to STEENVOORDE area leaving at 10 a.m. and detraining on arriving at ABEELE - STEENVOORDE Road 1 kilo south of ABEELE marched to camp about 3 mile N.W. of POPERINGHE. Tents & bivouacs & field provided for the Bn.	

Army Form C. 2118.

WAR DIARY
or
INTELLIGENCE SUMMARY.
(Erase heading not required.)

Instructions regarding War Diaries and Intelligence Summaries are contained in F. S. Regs., Part II. and the Staff Manual respectively. Title pages will be prepared in manuscript.

Place	Date	Hour	Summary of Events and Information	Remarks and references to Appendices
Camp near ABEELE	3rd Cont.		The Bde. issued orders that all tents must be struck at dawn. The Transport marched by road & arrived about 3pm.	
	4th		Bn stood to from 7am – 7.30am. Inspections carried out during the day. Training on a large scale not possible as the field occupied by the Battalion was under observation from Kemmel hill	
	5th		The Battalion moved to ATLANTIC CAMP near BUSSBOOM. B'chelu minimum Reserve remained in same Place. Camp consisted of huts at farm Rouxs. (3 coys in huts 1 coy & gun).	
ATLANTIC Camp.	6th		Patrols sent out to reconnoitre B's & Bttns of Right Bde (30th Comp or G Bde) & Left Bde (95th Bde) of the Division. The Bde was to take up a position in close Support. D coy was sent out to Brigade Res in front of OUDERDOM in the SWITCH line joining up with the FRENCH who are holding the line south of the Bn't Front. an was established	

WAR DIARY
or
INTELLIGENCE SUMMARY.
(Erase heading not required.)

Army Form C. 2118.

Place	Date	Hour	Summary of Events and Information	Remarks and references to Appendices
At Latrine Camp	7th		Inspections & training in vicinity of camp carried out during the morning. Accompany relieved D Coy in Switch Line in the afternoon. B & C Coys on working parties during the night digging new Switch Line North East of OUDERDOM.	
"	8th		Enemy attacked the French and 33rd Brit front Battery at dawn after the French had made an attack & drove the line back. Message received at about 9.20 am that the Bn was to compose Bde front was shown that the Bn was to take up a position in the VLAMERTINGHE LINE between HALLEBAST CORNER and a point 600x NE of HALLEBAST CORNER & would be prepared to make a deliberate counter attack if necessary. Bn then moved forward thro' via BUSSEBOOM to OUDERDOM interval of 100x between Platoons - Coys moved off in order C.B.D. in VLAMERTINGHE LINE C coy Road across to take up a position from + HALLEBAST CORNER & B coy to take up position from left of C coy to a point 300 yds NNE then point. D coy to Road function 300x NNE of the crossroad	

WAR DIARY
or
INTELLIGENCE SUMMARY.
(Erase heading not required.)

Army Form C. 2118.

Place	Date	Hour	Summary of Events and Information	Remarks and references to Appendices
			The Bn. moved forward via BUSSEBOOM + GOODMOET MILL C company with orders to take up a position from HALLEBAST CORNER to a point in the VLAMERTINGHE LINE 300 NNE of the crossroads + B coy from this point to a point 300 NNE of C coy left. D company a support position 300 in rear of B + C coy. The coys took up positions about 1.30 p.m. Bn. H.Q. moved forward to a dugout on the railway 400 south of OUDERDOM. The commanding officer + intelligence officer then went forward to reconnoitre the position for the VLAMERTINGHE LINE at 12 noon. A coy remained in this former position in the switch line near OUDERDOM. at 12.30 P.M. H.Q. moved forward again to a farm 600 NNW of ST HERTRETH HOEK at 3.30 pm orders were received that the attack. The Bn was to attack on the R.5 hrs south. The 5th Scottish Rifles on the left. The attack was to take place in conjunction with 98 Bde who were attacking on the left.	

WAR DIARY
or
INTELLIGENCE SUMMARY.
(Erase heading not required.)

Army Form C. 2118.

Instructions regarding War Diaries and Intelligence Summaries are contained in F. S. Regs., Part II. and the Staff Manual respectively. Title pages will be prepared in manuscript.

Place	Date	Hour	Summary of Events and Information	Remarks and references to Appendices
			The Bn was to form up near HALLEBAST CROSS ROADS & advance with the left flank in the HALLEBAST-VIERSTRAAT Rd on the right. Its task was to keep in touch with the French who were attacking at the same time. The Bn was to cross the ROZEN HILL BECK at 7pm & on an mt of the extent of the advance the Barrage was to continue until 7.15pm. The objective was the old front line system which had been taken by the enemy that morning. At 3.30 Orders were given that the Commanding Officer would meet Company Commanders at HALLEBAST CROSS ROADS at 5.15pm & that C.O's were to be found up on their present position at that Zero hour to move off immediately verbal orders were issued by the commanding officer. A Coy was given written orders know forward at once to HALLEBAST CORNER when further orders would be issued. At 5.15 The Commanding Officer met O.C's of B C & D Coys- explained the situation & gave orders for them to form up on Bastrall Trench South of HALLEBAST Cross Roads already known know forward at 6pm in this HALLEBAST-VIERSTRAAT Road– B Coy on right & C on the left in its left in that, HALLEBAST-VIERSTRAAT Road. D Coy was to advance 260 yds	

in rear of B & C coys. were to advance in Artillery formation
on receiving prearranged Coys. signal & advanced in artillery
at 6 p.m. B.C. & D coys. took up their position & as soon as
the road got clear of attacking formation up
formation as soon as the road got clear of attacking
position. A hurricane bombardment was put down on the attacker of
CRATER which in fact & a few casualties on B coy who had just
arrived.
The Commanding Officer then gave Capt Wyldbore (O.C. A coy) to move
forward in rear of D coy which he did
As soon as the leading Companies reached the ridge North of
ROZEN HILL BEEK the heavy barrage of Machine Gun fire
opened - A certain amount of Artillery fire opened but a position
barrage was not put down until A coy reached the objec-
-tive few casualties were inflicted by shell fire by our heavy
casualties occurred through Machine Gun fire.
The Company Commanders of A B & C coys were wounded almost

Immediately:-
In the advance B & C coys lost direction & went over to the right leaving a gap of about 700 yds on the left between the left flank of the 16th & the right of the 5th Seaforth Rifles. Movements of the leading companies. Got well across the ROZEN-HILLBECK this oring from heavy casualties from M.G. fire while crossing the stream were not able to take in to their position.

At about 9pm the same night the position was consolidated went of to ROZEN HILLBECK with 5th Lewis Guns on the far side of the stream. On the left, as touch could not be gained with the 5th Seaforth Rifles, a defensive flank was formed on the left which was covered by 4 Lewis Gun posts. The ground was very marshy & formed a very formidable obstacle.

At midnight 8th/9th Lt Col Draper & Lt Roll and a runner went out to try to find the companies as no message had been received from them. After leaving Batt HQ which was in a hut 150 yds west of BRANDEN BEEK Ey 14 nothing was ever heard.

Place	Date	Hour	Summary of Events and Information	Remarks and references to Appendices
	9th		Ttem - An unofficial report had been received at about 9 p.m. on the evening of 8/9 which said that the French & our corps were in their objective. This was noted the Coln. At about 7 am a cycle sketch was forwarded by Lt Lofsa who had taken command of the remnants of the Bgops in which he stated that there were only about 80 men left. Later a further report giving the exact disposition was forwarded. 	
	10th		Att- by Lt. the Bn was relieved by the Queens & took up a position in the KLANENTINGHE line - near the after the Bn withdrew to camp at RAILLEBOOM at 3pm - Total Casualties 16.Or KILLED. 184 wounded. 10. wounded missing. 36 missing Lt Col Drake oto } missing 2/Lt Bryans 2/Lt Wallace} wounded missing Lt Roth MC 2/Lt R.K.Mitchell} killed Lt Clay Lt F.B.Anderson Lt Hoshbrick } wounded 2/Lt Aglionby } wounded Lt Powell Lt REMINGTON	

Army Form C. 2118.

WAR DIARY
or
INTELLIGENCE SUMMARY.
(Erase heading not required.)

Place	Date	Hour	Summary of Events and Information	Remarks and references to Appendices
Marqueffles	MAY 11th		Marched to DIRTY BUCKET CORNER area very good camp in a wood. All men in huts.	
DIRTY BUCKET CORNER.	12th		Cleaning up during the morning. The Corps & Divt Commanders inspected the Bn also 5th Scottish Rifles on Parade & congratulated both Battalions on the fight of 8th & 9th. Parade Service after the Parade.	XXII
DIRTY BUCKET	13th	9.15 a.m. to 12.15 p.m.	Training carried out near the camp. S.B.R. Drill - Musketry - Handling of Arms - Close order drill - Lewis Gun & Signalling + Bombing Classes 9.15 - 12.15 p.m.	
	14th		Training carried out as on 13th.	
	15th		Training from 9 a.m. to 12 Noon. Baths in the afternoon. All men to have fun clean fired on range	
	16th		Training Parade as for 14th Lewis fun class fired under Bombing Officer	
	17th		under L.G. Officer. Bombing class fired under Bombing Officer. Practice Parade for Army Commander's Parade. Whole Bde formed up in mass in a field next to the Camp. ½ Rums drill carried out after the Parade.	
	18th		The Bn was inspected by 2nd Corps C & Southwd Strafe in Campbell	

WAR DIARY
or
INTELLIGENCE SUMMARY.
(Erase heading not required.)

Army Form C. 2118.

Place	Date	Hour	Summary of Events and Information	Remarks and references to Appendices
	18th contd		DIRTY BUCKET and marched back to camp at L.8.d.9.2. N. West of Poperinghe. Accomodated in huts + Bivvies. Improvements to camp carried out:- The Battalion before leaving DIRTY BUCKET camp at 4.15am moved in artillery formation to a point on ELVERDINGHE - POPERINGHE road near DAN HANGER DUMP. + arrived in new camp about 7.30am	
camp at L.8.d.9.2. Sheet 27	19th		Church parade in morning. Washing Equipments all Bu steel helmets painted for Army Commander's inspection parade.	
	20th		Draft of 36 O.R. arrived all young men always age 19 years. Brigadier inspects Draft in clean fatigue also inspected the transport at 7am. 2nd Army Commander (General Sir H. Plumer G.C.B. G.C.M.G. G.C.V.O) inspected the Bn. in a field near B.H.Q. The Bn paraded at 10.30am in Dill order + complemented the Bn on its fighting at METEREN 7-8-9th of May at the NEMMEL BEER Rds on its fighting at HOUT KERQUE at 5pm. + accomodated in a canvas camp in wood near the aerodrome and near the Bois de ST ACAIRE.	

Army Form C. 2118.

WAR DIARY
or
INTELLIGENCE SUMMARY.
(Erase heading not required.)

Instructions regarding War Diaries and Intelligence Summaries are contained in F. S. Regs., Part II. and the Staff Manual respectively. Title pages will be prepared in manuscript.

Place	Date	Hour	Summary of Events and Information	Remarks and references to Appendices
Bois de St ACAIRE.	21st		Very good ranges. Bayonet fighting course put near the camp.	
	22nd		A Coy firing on the range at 6am. other Companies Physical training before breakfast 6.15am + B Coy on range after Breakfast at 8.15am. Remainder of Battalion Physical training Bayonet fighting Musketry, close order drill S.B.R. Drill artillery formation 8.15am to 11.30am. Lt Colonel G. Wingate, M.C. T.D. Highland Light Infantry assumed Command of the Battalion.	
			9.30am to 12.30pm. Same to render as for 21st B coy fighting on range. The Commanding Officer inspected all Companies in marching order. Lewis gun, Lysolling, Bombing classes carried at. Lewis guns fired in the afternoon under Lewis gun Officer. Junior N.C.O.s paraded under Regimental Sgt Major for instruction at 5.30am. The Band played on Parade at 7th Brigade R.A.F. at 6.20 p.m. A C coy at Bath from 4pm to 8pm.	

Army Form C. 2118.

WAR DIARY
or
INTELLIGENCE SUMMARY.
(Erase heading not required.)

Place	Date	Hour	Summary of Events and Information	Remarks and references to Appendices
Bdes	23rd		"A" Coys at Baths in the morning. "C" Company fired on Range at 6 a.m. Lewis gunners fired in the range from 9.30 a.m. to 12.30. Usual parade for rest of the morning. All Coys fired on the Range during the afternoon.	
	24th	8.30 am to 10 am	Beer at Baths	
		10 am to 11.30 am	"D" Coy at Baths	
			NCOs & Platoon commanders paraded under RSM during the morning for instruction in fitting up Equipment.	
			The Bn marched to Bivonas South of POPERINGHE Station as relief	
		3.40 a.m.	Bde marched 3.40 a.m. Very wet trench - Heavy rain the whole way. Breakfasts on arrival in new area.	
POPERINGHE	25th	4 a.m.	At 4 a.m. the Battalion worked on the BLUE SUPPORT LINE, forming part of the POPERINGHE defences making up the parapet & parados to 2nd Bn & Coys Battalion under the supervision of the 11th Field Coy. R.E. and 18th Middlesex pioneers. In the afternoon the S.B. R's of the battalion were inspected at the Bde gas hut. 2 practices were fired by all Coys on the 30% range beside Bde HQ	

WAR DIARY
INTELLIGENCE SUMMARY

Place	Date	Hour	Summary of Events and Information	Remarks and references to Appendices
POPERINGHE	26th		The same working parties as for the 25th except that 2 Coys worked under 11th Lt Coy R.E. 2 Coys under 18th Middlesex. Training in Lewis Gun was undertaken by the Nos 1 of the guns & all the men in the Battalion from 2 & 3. voluntary Rcs. & bof. service. The following officers joined Capt J.K. Baker, officer J.B.P. Brown 2/Lieut J. Garrity. A draft of 64 arrived. Large number of officers very good draft	
	27th		The Commanding Officer inspected the Battn in full marching order. Lewis Gun was fired by every man of A and D Coys. The usual parades for specialists were carried out.	
	28th		A Coy proceeded to DIRTY BUCKET CORNER on a working party to work to 2nd Corps battern YELLOW LINE. The remainder of the battalion carried out the usual instructional parades, special stress being laid on the necessity of all men firing the Lewis Gun. Congratulatory memo. was received from C.R.E. on the work of the battalion. Divisional + Brigade Commanders added their appreciation. 5 Bars to M.M. and 9 Military Medals for the KEMMEL BECK battle were notified in Corps routine orders. A Coy proceeded to RUBROUCK for musketry till the 31st	

Army Form C. 2118.

WAR DIARY
or
INTELLIGENCE SUMMARY.
(Erase heading not required.)

Instructions regarding War Diaries and Intelligence Summaries are contained in F. S. Regs., Part II. and the Staff Manual respectively. Title pages will be prepared in manuscript.

Place	Date	Hour	Summary of Events and Information	Remarks and references to Appendices
POPERINGHE	29th		At 5 a.m. A & B Coys under direction of 222 & 15th Coy R.E. & C Coy under 174th Middlesex commenced work on the BLUE SUPPORT LINE making up the parapet and parados to 2nd korps pattern. In the afternoon H.Q. details received instruction on the firing of the Lewis Gun.	
	30th		Working parties as for the 29th.	
	31st		The usual training programme was carried out. The HOPOUTRE BATHS were allotted to the battalion in the afternoon. D Coy marched proceeded to RUBROUCK for musketry relieving C Coy. The following awards were notified. MILITARY CROSS Capt. R.M. Miller, Captain G.A. Ryons. D.C.M. 41042 A/Cpl McIvor. Lieut. L.R. Wigan. (attd.) all being award to WESTERN BATTn.	

E.M. Ringrose
Lieut. Colonel,
Commanding, 17th Bn. the Sam'wicans.

The Cameroons

1 Scottish Rifles

Vol 47

WAR DIARY or INTELLIGENCE SUMMARY.

Place	Date	Hour	Summary of Events and Information	Remarks and references to Appendices
POPERINGHE	1/6/18		Training	
"	2/6/18		Minimum Reserve proceeded to Camp (L.7.a.9.6.) to pitch tents and prepare for Battalion arrival	
"	3/6/18	5 am	Battalion march to Camp (L.7.a.9.6.) BOLLEZEELE (Via D. Coy at Range - L.17.d.0.6. - L.11.c.7.8 - ZWYNLAND BREWERY - L.11.a.7.5. to L.7.a.9.6. - L.17.d.0.6. - L.11.c.7.8 - Route - G.8.a.7.7. - Railway to G.7.6.1.	
L.7.a.9.6	4/6/18	2.15 pm	"D" rejoined Battalion Training - Bn Parade 7.30 AM - 8.30 AM Musketry } 8.30 AM - 10.30 AM Bayonet fighting Gas Drill	
"	5/6/18		Training as for 4th	
"	6/6/18		Training - Close Order Drill Musketry P.T. & B.F. Gas Drill } 8 AM - 11.45 AM Specialist Classes	

HS.M
5 sheet

Army Form C. 2118.

WAR DIARY
or
INTELLIGENCE SUMMARY.
(Erase heading not required.)

SECRET.

Instructions regarding War Diaries and Intelligence Summaries are contained in F. S. Regs., Part II. and the Staff Manual respectively. Title pages will be prepared in manuscript.

Place	Date	Hour	Summary of Events and Information	Remarks and references to Appendices
L.7.8.9.6.	7/6/18	—	Generally preparing for move	
		7.30 PM	Battalion moved to relief of 1st Bn. The Middlesex Regiment of 16th Infantry Brigade (Support Bn.) BELGIAN BATTERY CORNER. "D" Company relieved one Company of the York & Lancs. Regt. Battalion moved in three trains from PONT REMY Station (Ligne Railway) L.2r.d. entrained & detrained at MACHINE GUN SIDING (N.12.b.)	
BELGIAN BATTERY CORNER	8/6/18	—	Heavy Gas shelling. Casualties —	
"	9/6/18	—	2nd Lieut. A.M.R. Steel & 2 O.R. Killed in Action Capt. P.N. GARDINER 2/Lt. G.R.B. CLARK (Died 13/6/18) } Wounded 24 O.R.	
	10/4/18	—		
LINE	11/6/18	—	Battalion moved into the Line Casualties — 2nd Lieut. W. CHAMBERS } Wounded P.R. McARTHUR 6 O.R.	

Army Form C. 2118.

WAR DIARY
or
INTELLIGENCE-SUMMARY.   SECRET.

(Erase heading not required.)

Instructions regarding War Diaries and Intelligence Summaries are contained in F. S. Regs., Part II. and the Staff Manual respectively. Title pages will be prepared in manuscript.

Place	Date	Hour	Summary of Events and Information	Remarks and references to Appendices
LINE	JUNE 12	—	Casualties — 8 O.R. Wounded	
"	13	—	"	
"	14	—	"	
"	15	—	12 Reinforcements. Battalion moved back to ERIE CAMP.	
ERIE CAMP	16	—	Working parties on Reserve Lines	
"	17	—	"	
"	18	—	"	
"	19	—	"	
"	20	—	Battalion moved into the Line to relieve 1st Bn. The Middlesex Regiment. Major Hon. H. RITCHIE D.S.O. Joined the Battalion (Minimum Reserve)	
LINE	21	—	Casualties — 1 O.R. Killed in Action	
"	22	—	53 Reinforcements. 2/Lt. W BROWNLIE ⎱ Joined the Battalion " J. McDONALD ⎰ " A HENDERSON	

Army Form C. 2118.

WAR DIARY
or
INTELLIGENCE SUMMARY.
(Erase heading not required.)

SECRET

Instructions regarding War Diaries and Intelligence Summaries are contained in F.S. Regs., Part II. and the Staff Manual respectively. Title pages will be prepared in manuscript.

Place	Date	Hour	Summary of Events and Information	Remarks and references to Appendices
LINE.	JUNE 23.	-	Casualties - 25th. 4 killed, 1 O.R. wounded, 15 O.R. wounded	
"	24.	-	-	
"	25.	-	Casualties - Captain J.K. BAKER wounded. 2/Lt. C.W. WOODS to hospital & since classed Wounded (Gas). Lieut HIGAN } to hospital. " WHITE. 2/Lt GARRETTY	
"	26.	-	130 Reinforcements. Col. WINGATE to "B" Echelon sick. Major RITCHIE assumed Command.	
"	27.	-	Col. WINGATE to Corps Rest Station. Captain BECNER to leave from Minimum Reserve. 2/Lt D. McINTYRE ⎫ " J.T. WHITSON ⎬ joined the Battalion. " J. STEVENSON ⎭	

WAR DIARY
or
INTELLIGENCE SUMMARY.

Army Form C. 2118.

SECRET

(Erase heading not required.)

Place	Date	Hour	Summary of Events and Information	Remarks and references to Appendices
LINE	JUNE 27		Minimum Reserve moved to outskirts of WATOU	
"	29		2/Lt. R. HERBERT taken on Strength at Divisional Wing.	
"	30		Battalion relieved by 9th Bn. (S.R.) H.L.I. move to BRANDHOEK Area (Divisional Reserve)	
			Bn. H. Qrs. G. 11. d. 30.15.	
			"A" Coy. " G. 11. d. 20. 30. In camp	
			"B" Coy. " G. 18. b. 50. 60. {2 platoons Green Line {2 platoons Yellow "	
			"C" Coy. " do.	
			"D" Coy. " G. 18. d. 20. 70. In Yellow Line.	

H. Mitchie Major
Commanding THE CAMERONIANS

1st Cameronians

Army Form C.-2118.

SECRET

Vol 4 8

WAR DIARY
or
INTELLIGENCE SUMMARY.
(Erase heading not required.)

H.H.M
5 sheets

Place	Date	Hour	Summary of Events and Information	Remarks and references to Appendices
BRANDHOEK	July 1.	—	Battalion in Divisional Reserve. HdQrs G.11.d.35.15. Baths. Conference of Officers w/ French Routine. Draft of 22 Other Ranks joined Minimum Reserve.	
"	2	7.0 11.30 AM	'B','C' & 'D' Coys provide Working Parties on the GREEN LINE 'A' Coy - P.T., Squad Mounting, Musketry &c. 26 Other Ranks joined the Battalion	
"	3	7.0 11.30 AM	50 Men from each Company, Working Party on the GREEN LINE. Remainder of 'A' Coy training as on 2nd inst. Remainder of 'B','C' & 'D' Coys improving local trenches. Captain CRAIG & 55 Other Ranks from Minimum Reserve 60 " " " " " "	
"	4	—	General training by Companies O/C's, 'B','C' & 'D' Coys reconnoitred line to be taken over by the Battalion. Minimum Reserve moved from WATOU Area to POPERINGHE Area	

Army Form C. 2118.

WAR DIARY
or
INTELLIGENCE SUMMARY.
(Erase heading not required.)

Instructions regarding War Diaries and Intelligence Summaries are contained in F. S. Regs., Part II. and the Staff Manual respectively. Title pages will be prepared in manuscript.

Place	Date	Hour	Summary of Events and Information	Remarks and references to Appendices
BRANDHOEK	JULY 5	7.0	'B' 'C' & 'D' Coys provide Working Party on the GREEN LINE	
		11.30 AM	'D' Coy - Tactical Scheme	
		8.30 PM	'C' Coy move off to relieve 'A' Coy, 21 Bn., Rl. Bde., CANAL (9th K.L.I.)	
		9 PM	'D' & 'B' Coys move off to relieve 3 Coys of Rl. Bn., Rl. Bde., CANAL (2nd R.S.N.)	
			'A' Coy of 2/R.o.S.N. being relieved by 1 Coy of 1st Bn. The Queens. 1 Coy 5 R. Bn Scottish Rifles take over Rl Coy G.H.Q. 1 & 2.	
CANAL	6	—	4 Officers & 6 O.R. United States Army (30th Div) are attached for instruction for 48 hours.	
			Rl. Support Coy relieve Coy of the 5th S.R. on G.H.Q. 1 & 2.	
"	7	—	"	
"	8	—	4 Officers & 6 O.R. U.S.A. left	
"	9	—	4 " 4 " " " Joined } the Battalion	

WAR DIARY
or
INTELLIGENCE SUMMARY.

(Erase heading not required.)

Army Form C. 2118.

Place	Date	Hour	Summary of Events and Information	Remarks and references to Appendices
CAMP 6	July 10	-	4 Officers 4 O.R. left } the Battalion (U.S.A. personnel)	
			4 " 5 O.R. joined	
	11	-	Draft of 29 Other Ranks joined Minimum Reserve	
			2/Lt CHAMBERS & HERBERT " "	
			Pte McFADYEN killed 1 O.R. wounded.	
	12	-	Lt. While rejoined from Hospital	
			Pte C WILSON N° 41504 killed in Action 1 O.R. wounded	
			4 Officers 5 O.R. U.S.A. left	
			Lt ROGER + 2/Lt WOODS rejoined Minimum Reserve from Hospital	
	13	-	1 O.R. wounded	
	14	-		
	15	-	Relieved by 16th Bn K.R.R.C. the Battalion went back to EPIS FARM Area	
			3 O.R. wounded.	
BRANDHOEK	16	-	Inspection by Company Commanders	
			1 O.R. wounded	

Army Form C. 2118.

WAR DIARY
or
INTELLIGENCE SUMMARY.
(Erase heading not required.)

Instructions regarding War Diaries and Intelligence Summaries are contained in F.S. Regs., Part II. and the Staff Manual respectively. Title pages will be prepared in manuscript.

Place	Date	Hour	Summary of Events and Information	Remarks and references to Appendices
BRANDHOEK	July 17	—	Inspection of Coys by Commanding Officer. Major R.D. HUNTER rejoined the Battalion. Draft of 250 O.R. transferred from N.L.I. 2/Lt WEIR rejoins from II Corps Works Battalion	
"	18	—	Working Parties in the GREEN & YELLOW Lines. Major J.R. JACK took up command of the Battalion	
"	19	3-30 PM	Aeroplane Contact practice. 2/Lt COL WINGATE proceeded to report to the War Office.	
"	20	—	2/Lt WIGAN rejoined from Hospital. Major JACK relieved Major RITCHIE who joines Minimum Reserve. Battalion moved into Support (THE RAVINE) relieving 1st Bn. Middlesex	
CANAL	21	—	The Battalion spent a quiet day in the Support lines. Working Parties were forked by A and B Companies after dark	
"	22	"	Working Parties provided by C and D Companies	

WAR DIARY
or
INTELLIGENCE SUMMARY.
(Erase heading not required.)

Army Form C. 2118.

Place	Date	Hour	Summary of Events and Information	Remarks and references to Appendices
CANAL	23	-	2/Lt YOUNG + 2/Lt McARTHUR joined. Minimum Reserve	
"	24	-	"	
"	25	-	"	
"	26	-	3 O.R. wounded by Aeroplane Bomb at 'D' Echelon. Battalion relieved 1/1 Bn The Queens in the Rt Sector of the Rt Bde Front. 'C' and 'D' Companies in front line, A support and 'B' reserve	
"	27	-	The battalion spent a quiet day in the line	
"	28	-	As for 27th	
"	29	10.45PM	A prisoner was captured by 'C' Company, 'D' Company 90 R's wounded. Prisoner belonged to a fresh formation, Reform eng.	
"	30	-	On the night of 30/31 the battalion was relieved by 2nd Dorset Regiment and took up position in the GREEN LINE in Divisional Reserve.	
"	31	-	Company spent the day cleaning up. Captain R. Beeston admitted to hospital. Captain R.J. Gents taking over as Adjt	

31/4/18.

10th Bn. The Cameronians
(Scottish Rifles)

SECRET

1st Bn THE CAMERONIANS
1 Scottish Regt
Vol 4

Army Form C. 2118.

WAR DIARY
or
INTELLIGENCE SUMMARY

(Erase heading not required.)

Instructions regarding War Diaries and Intelligence Summaries are contained in F.S. Regs., Part II. and the Staff Manual respectively. Title pages will be prepared in manuscript.

45.11 Oct wks

Place	Date	Hour	Summary of Events and Information	Remarks and references to Appendices
VLAMERTINGHE.				
GREEN LINE	Aug 1st 1918		A working party was found by A,B and C Companies for work on Green Line.	
	Aug 2nd		The battalion marched off at 7.0 A.M. to a field WEST OF POPERINGHE - VLAMERTINGHE Road and practiced an attack. Owing to heavy rain in the forenoon further parades were cancelled and officers delivered lectures to their Companies.	
	Aug 3rd		Two Companies A & D provided working parties for labour on Green line. Revolver practice was carried out by officers under 2nd in Command.	
	Aug 4th		Fifty men per Coy were found for work on Green line. Voluntary Church Service were held. In the evening the battalion relieved 1st Middlesex Regt. in Belt Barn Left Sub-sector Canal Sector. Two platoons of 3rd & 120th Regt USA were handed over to each Coy	
	Aug 5th		Quiet day in line. 2 Lieut Lebert admitted to hospital sick.	
	Aug 6th		Quiet day in line. 1 O.R. wounded.	
	Aug 7th		Commanding Officer attended lecture on training at TERDINGHEM	
	Aug 8th		1 O.R. wounded.	
	Aug 9th		On night of Aug 9th/10th "B" Coy relieved "A" Coy in front line. 1 O.R. wounded.	

WAR DIARY
or
INTELLIGENCE SUMMARY.

(Erase heading not required.)

Army Form C. 2118.

Place	Date	Hour	Summary of Events and Information	Remarks and references to Appendices
	Aug 10th		Night of 10th/11th D Coy relieved Americans on left of B Coy. 2 O.R.s killed	
			Captain Millar rejoined from leave	
	Aug 11th		2 O.R.s wounded 2/Lt Henderson to hospital sick	
	Aug 12		2nd Lt Grant wounded 2 O.R.s wounded & believed killed 10 O.R. wounded	
			1 Lt missing 3 O.R.s wounded	
	Aug 13			
	Aug 14		On night of 14th/15th Battn was relieved by 16th R.R.C. After relief moving back to Yellow line. B.H.Q. at CATTERICK CAMP.	
			4 O.R.s wounded	
	Aug 15th		No infantry took place in morning. At about 1.30 P.M. Orders were received that Bn would be relieved from Div. Reserve by 1/119 American Regt about 9.15 P.M. After relief Bn marched to RAINSFORD CAMP Sheet 27/K 12 b 6.4. Arrived about 1.30 A.M. on 16th RAINSFORD CAMP Nr PROVEN. Route through PUPERINGHE.	

WAR DIARY
or
INTELLIGENCE SUMMARY

Army Form C. 2118.

Place	Date	Hour	Summary of Events and Information	Remarks and references to Appendices
BAINSFORD	16		Church parade the minimum Reserve joined the Battn	
	17		Training was carried out by Companies during morning. Bath in afternoon. Gift from a lady was allocated to Coys and	
			to substitutes of contact Pneumonia. Band the Coys during the evening. 2/Lt. C.S. CONNELL. M.R.C. U.S.A. attached Capt. LYONS. R.A.M.C.	
	18		Training was carried out by Companies followed [by]	
			Church parade	4½ miles
	19		About 10 am Battn marched to MENDING # E.M. and entrained for WATTEN as marched to NORD LEUVLINGHEM 4.8 miles while arrangements were being made for the night. The Battn marched at 9 pm for LICQUES leaving about 4 OM. A. B. at CIREBOURNE. "B" LE COMMUNE C and D in LICQUES. March about 11 miles.	
LICQUES	20			
	21		Coys carried out training in training area for 9:30 am to 12-20 P.M.	

WAR DIARY
or
INTELLIGENCE SUMMARY.

Army Form C. 2118.

Place	Date	Hour	Summary of Events and Information	Remarks and references to Appendices
LIEQUES	22ⁿᵈ		Batt⁴ were on range from 8am to 12-30pm. In afternoon Brig Gen Duggan delivered a lecture on training to all officers and platoon commanders of the Batt.	
	23ʳᵈ		Training carried out from 7-30 to 11-30 on training area	
	24ᵗʰ		2 Coys on Range. W & X LIEQVES, two companies training.	
	25ᵗʰ		Church Parade CofE and RC only in Church and Lecture Hall. A party of 2 O.R's went to MALO for the day. Shrapnel performed in the evening.	
	26ᵗʰ	1am	Batt⁴ received warning orders to be prepared to move. Train at short notice. During afternoon billets, baths left to BAYENGHEM. Batt⁴ left about 5PM	

Appendix A

Captain R. M. Miller — M.C.
Lieut. C. R. Wigan — M.C.
Lieut. W. D. Roger — M.C.

Sgt. G. Forwood — M.M.
Cpl. W. McGregor — M.M and bar
Sgt. T. Harrison — M.M.
Pte. J. O'Donnell — M.M.

WAR DIARY
or
INTELLIGENCE SUMMARY.
(Erase heading not required.)

Army Form C. 2118.

Place	Date	Hour	Summary of Events and Information	Remarks and references to Appendices
	26		Arrived about 9-30 PM. 12 miles march in Review	
	27		Billeting party left for IVERGNY	
	28		"B" Company entrained at WISERNES at 7 am the remainder of Batt's entrained at 10-4. Detrained also at PREVENT when Batt's marched to Billets at IVERGNY. 10 ays march about 12 miles. Inspections were carried out in Company	
IVERGNY	29			
	30		The Batt's marched to a field on LE SOUICH where the Divisional Commander conferred medal ribands after which the Bde marched past the General and returned to their billets. List of recipients attached. Appendix A.	
	31		Coy carried out training during the morning in confield in thin hills.	

R Smith A/Lieut Colonel
Commanding 1/5th The Cameronians

WAR DIARY of 1st Bn. The Cameron Highlanders

INTELLIGENCE SUMMARY
Army Form C. 2118.

Place	Date	Hour	Summary of Events and Information	Remarks and references to Appendices
IVERGNY	1.9.18		Bn. Series at IVERGNY — Baths at LUCHEUX.	
do.	2nd.		Battalion Tactical Exercise.	
do.	3rd.		Brigade Tactical Scheme.	
do.	4th/5th.		Battalion Tactical Exercise — Advancing with tanks. Lieut J.R. Maclean Hospital. ½ limbers to represent tanks.	
do.	6th.		Brigade Tactical Scheme near LE SOUICH; C.O. & 74 officers attended Tank Demonstration at WAVRANS.	
do.	7th.		Tactical Exercises — Battalion Concert at night with No 3 A.A. Workshops.	
do.	8th.		Divine Service — Lt Col. Jack RSF proceeded to assume Command. 28th Infantry Brigade. Capt. R.B. Hunter RSF. proceeded as Insp. in C. to 9th Gordon Rifles. Lieut G.R. Wilson M.C. assumed duties of Adjutant. 2/Lt Hubert reid' from hospital. Captain J.M. Forsyth & 2/Lt. W.S. McDonald arrived as reinforcements.	
do.	9th.		Football Match for nd plae Canteen Committee.	
do.			Baths at LUCHEUX — Rain hindered training, which had to carried on indoors	
do.	10th to 12th		General training 11th Capt. T. Kubwood MC left over duties as a.a. Comund.	
	13th		General training — G.O.C's Conference.	

WAR DIARY
or
INTELLIGENCE SUMMARY

Army Form C. 2118

Place	Date	Hour	Summary of Events and Information	Remarks and references to Appendices
WERGNY	Nov 14th		General training. Bn embused at 8.30 a.m. on LE SOUICH road for ETRICOURT	
ETRICOURT	15th		Bn arrived 6 a.m. and encamped till. Marched up at 7.15 p.m. and relieved 7th Leicesters in support near HEUDICOURT.	
V.21 v 22	16th		Bn relieved in support moved back to V. 21 d v 22 - 57 c. Casualties for day - 15 OR Wounded.	
V. 17 v 20	17th		Cleaning up etc.	
	18th		Bn moved to trenches at V.17.	
V 20	19th		Bn moved up and encamped at W 20. at 7.30 p.m. Bn moved to line. BHQ in V 20. b. 3.3. A + B Coys in front line (on sunken road running through (X 14 d - X 20 b + d) "C" Coy in support - "D" Coy in Reserve.	
	20th		Preparations for attack tomorrow — 2/Rt DLI We Remainder Wounded. Attack by 33rd Division — 19th Bde on Right — 98 te Brigade on left 175th Bde (98th Division) on right of 15th Inf. Bde. Attack of 15th Bde carried out by 1st Queens on Right + the Bn on left Sth Ro. Rifles in Reserve. Objectives — 175 Inf. Bde: DADOS LOOP — 19th Inf. Bde: — X 22 d. 5. 7. X 22 Central. to road about V 22. 2. 3. 0. thence along GLOSTER Road	

WAR DIARY
or
INTELLIGENCE SUMMARY.
(Erase heading not required.)

Army Form C. 2118.

Place	Date	Hour	Summary of Events and Information	Remarks and references to Appendices
To X roads X.15.d.9.9. (inclusive)	21st		At 5.40 a.m. Bn: attacked front with orders to machine gun fire and were held up by uncut wire. A and B Companies front line D. Suffolk & Reserve "C" Company were sent forward soon after commencement of attack, but were unable to get on. Major Ritchie then went forward with remnants & two platoons but was wounded in MEATH LANE. The remnants of battalion collected and organised in MEATH LANE under the two remaining officers 2nd Lt Young & Lieut Stewart, wounded and otherwise wounded & joined Battalion after dark.	

WAR DIARY or INTELLIGENCE SUMMARY

Army Form C. 2118.

Place	Date	Hour	Summary of Events and Information	Remarks and references to Appendices
	21st		Casualties for tour —	
			Captain W.T. Brait } Killed in action	
			2/Lt. J.Y. Sassoon }	
			2/Lt. J.F. Wells }	
			2/Lt. R.R. MacArthur }	
			2/Lt. D. McLean }	
			2/Lt. A.J. Clark }	
			2/Lt. H.G. McDonald }	
			Major Hon. H. Ritchie DSO }	
			Capt. H. Lindsay }	
			2/Lt. J. R.A. Brown } Wounded	
			2/Lt. W. Braynlie }	
			2/Lt. J.T. Whittet }	
			2/Lt. D. McMillan }	
			2/Lt. D. Henderson }	
			2/Lt. J. McDonald }	
			2/Lt. C.D. Mardow }	
			37 OR Killed in action 23 OR Missing — 15= OR Wounded.	
Villers au Bois			Bn. Relieved by 16th Bn. R.R.R.C. & moved back to trenches	
	24th		in front of wood at V.17.	
	25th		Cleaning up — re-organising etc.	
	26th		Refitting — Clothing deficiencies.	
			Training — change of Divisional Reserve.	
			Bund disbanded & men employed in relief of various staff	

WAR DIARY
or
INTELLIGENCE SUMMARY.

Army Form C. 2118.

(Erase heading not required.)

Place	Date	Hour	Summary of Events and Information	Remarks and references to Appendices
N.17.	27th		To OR 7 Officers (Lieut. C. Gemmel) received	
X.13	28th		Bn. moved at 5 X.13 with intention of forming	
			up & sent in case of retirement. A and B Coys in	
			CAVALRY SUPPORT, C D CRICKET and FOOTBALL Trench. B⁴ was	
			under half an hours notice to move forward and secured	
			the line of CANAL.	
	29th		Battalion remains in a state of readiness to move	
	30th		a/Capt J.B. Maclean appointed minimum Reserve fire before	
			2OR to Lapride Gow	

John Kirkwood
Major
Commanding 1Bn. The Camerons

WAR DIARY or INTELLIGENCE SUMMARY

Army Form C. 2118.

1st Cameronians
1 Scottish Rifles

Place	Date	Hour	Summary of Events and Information	Remarks and references to Appendices
VAUCHELLES FARM	1/10/18		Bn in same position as yesterday. Lieut Stelling during night — 2 Casualties in B Coy — Bn on 2 hrs notice	
	2/10/18		Bn remained in same position — the Bodies of the undermentioned Officers, who fell in action on 21/9/18 were recovered & conducted from Battn and were buried at Dominion Cemetery :— Capt McCraig, 2/Lieut Black, 2/Lieut McLaurin, 2/Lieut Kearns, 2/Lieut Carey.	
	3/10/18		Bn moved into front line relieving 16/100 S Syl Bde. C Coy not in line - On R & L, C & D Coys. B Coy in reserve. B Coy in support. D Coy in support. We made every Coy & the Officers on to Coys in this Junk. PM Coys were sent out to reconnoitre & gaining ground till after dawn, and on return fell over 2nd and gaining ground till after dawn.	

Army Form C. 2118.

WAR DIARY
or
INTELLIGENCE SUMMARY.
(Erase heading not required.)

Place	Date	Hour	Summary of Events and Information	Remarks and references to Appendices
CANAL DE L'ESCAUT	4/10/18		At Dawn, under cover of mist, strong patrols endeavoured to secure bridgeheads across CANAL between ORSINVAL HONNECOURT, but, owing to heavy M.G. fire, were unable to force a passage. They were however successful in securing good points of observation close up to CANAL BANK, from which valuable information was obtained throughout the day.	
			The enemy showed a heavy artillery activity about 8 a.m. and M.G. barrage on right front of Bn.	
	5/10/18		At attempt to cross CANAL was taken up by M.G. fire during evening but it was not until 10th October that foot after dawn we were able to cross and secure Bridgehead. Wheeled O.P.s & T. M.S. in front of the Bn. were effective in warning & fixing line front of the...	

WAR DIARY
or
INTELLIGENCE SUMMARY.

Army Form C. 2118.

Place	Date	Hour	Summary of Events and Information	Remarks and references to Appendices
OSSUS.	5/10/18	A.M.	there and also got across CANAL in centre of Bn. front. Accompanied only by two runners, having realised that the enemy were retiring, they pushed forward & reconnoitred as far as KINGSTON QUARRY, where they found KINGSTON QUARRY, a remnant of foot not yet quite cold. Returning at once to nearest Coy. HQrs they notified Bn H.Qrs. Strong patrols were at once pushed over from each Coy. with instructions to secure the western road which covered the CANAL where all days necessary own recept to time. Bde HQrs were notified at once. Bn orders were confirmed, a frontage from Kingston Quarry to PUTNEY being allotted to Bn. Bn. HQ in our left, being notified that we were now also in passage from C.HQ nearest to QUARRY + KAPOG WOOD.	

WAR DIARY
or
INTELLIGENCE SUMMARY.

Army Form C. 2118.

Place	Date	Hour	Summary of Events and Information	Remarks and references to Appendices
KINGSTON QUARRY.	5/10/18	A.M.	According to O.O. Corps were in position. Bn. HQ moved to KINGSTON QUARRY and along patrols sent out forward to each Coy. Those reached RICHMOND QUARRY, BASKET WOOD, & LA TERRIERE, meeting only slight opposition from enemy, but lost at LA TERRIERE E. of Indians owing to our own artillery fire. Coy had been ordered not to advance beyond the Bn. Line on receipt of Patrol Reports. KINGSTON RD. Info. on receipt of which orders had been received to advance and permission was received to advance and occupy HINDENBURG LINE from RICHMOND WOOD to LA TERRIERE (exclusive). This was	
HINDENBURG LINE		P.M.	done & a line of outposts established in front. Total casualties during operations — 10. O.R. The excellent work of the Bn. Patrols during the operations was specially commended by Brigadier.	

WAR DIARY or INTELLIGENCE SUMMARY

Army Form C. 2118.

Place	Date	Hour	Summary of Events and Information	Remarks and references to Appendices
HINDENBURG LINE	4/10/18		The Bn. remained in HINDENBURG LINE in CORPS RESERVE. The Divisional Training Team appeared at By 17th & 18th Divisions. Wire training was carried out.	
	5/10/18		Same position. Bath received congratulatory tele. Divisional Comdr. on its fine work & for being first unit over CANAL.	
LE CATELET MARCOING	6/10/18		Same position. Lt. Col. Hon. D. Pelham D.S.O. returned & took over command from Major J. Harwood who proceeded to Mil. Reserve. Battn. moved at 1700 hrs to LE CATELET — MAUROY LINE.	
	9/10/18		Brigade ordered to advance through 38th Div. on CLARY, via AUBENCHEUL — VILLERS OUTREAUX — MALINCOURT. BATTN in RESERVE with 5th C.G. B/ & 1st Queen's in front. Advance started at 0200 hrs.	

WAR DIARY or INTELLIGENCE SUMMARY

Place	Date	Hour	Summary of Events and Information	Remarks and references to Appendices
DEVERIES	2/10/18		Slight opposition being encountered the Bde advanced rapidly through MAIRCOURT to CLARY which was captured & cleared by 0030 hrs. The Bn moved from DEHERIES to 1811 PM at 0001 M (O.34.a.90) at 2h pm. The Bn advanced through of OVIENS with orders to advance through BERTRY-TROISVILLES to NEUVILLY.	
BERTRY			BERTRY was reached & occupied after slight opposition but a heavy barrage was put down on Ridge E. of the village. Over 1500 Civilians were in the Ridge, on a reconnce the troops were met in trenches at home. The advance was continued towards TROISVILLES. This ridge was strongly held & strongly affected artillery fire. The BERTRY came under heavy M.G. & artillery fire, and several casualties were incurred.	

WAR DIARY or INTELLIGENCE SUMMARY

Army Form C. 2118.

Place	Date	Hour	Summary of Events and Information	Remarks and references to Appendices
TROISVILLES	9/10/18		The Batn. moved forward to the outskirts of TROISVILLES where the left Flank was held up by rifle & M.G. fire from a strong point. The post which was long afterwards to be seen held by 20/30 men & 2 M.G's was attacked by two men of the Batn. Pte Williams Peel, the two men indicated they were the point to Pymly. returned taking two wounded prisoner. It was on this information the Battn advanced & took up on the whole line two advanced platoons & held line consolidated running 9 thro' G.28.c.9. retiring enemy towards L.T. Baker advanced 3 platoons of A Coy under sight L.T. Baker advanced and NEUVILLY where heavy MG fire was encountered and Capt Baker killed. The rec'd movement continued was forced to fall back owing to casualties hindering operation. The Coy. Rifle coy again advanced during the advance, the Batn. two advanced were & mtrs. west of an country fighting most of its way. The noise of enemy fighting most of its way. The manner in which, on the closing stages of the advance, Rifled targets offering to the not settling of the advance, Battens especially by Mc. from an accurate M.G. position

WAR DIARY
or
INTELLIGENCE SUMMARY.

(Erase heading not required.)

Army Form C. 2118.

Instructions regarding War Diaries and Intelligence Summaries are contained in F. S. Regs., Part II. and the Staff Manual respectively. Title pages will be prepared in manuscript.

Place	Date	Hour	Summary of Events and Information	Remarks and references to Appendices
TROISVILLES	12/10/18	A.M.	Bn in outskirts in front of TROISVILLES. Got Bde. advanced through outskirts at dawn. Major J. Kirkwood M.C. took over command and [Lt.] Blake to hospital wounded.	
		P.M.	Bn moved back into Billets in TROISVILLES, & proceeded to reorganize.	
	12/10/18		Same Billets + Bn reorganizing + parties of Bn at K.20 digging looks.	
MALINCOURT	13/10/18		Bn moved back across country to MALINCOURT where remnants of Reserve reported. Lt. Wyatt & Lt. Mills + 9th Battn. joined Battn.	
	13/10/18		Battn. paraded for inspection by G.O.C. Division who congratulated all ranks in the splendid work done, made special reference to the work of patrols on 5th & 11th Octr., & to the courage & endurance of the men who had no moment to rest, to every rank under him, on the 9th inst. A. Bourn Capt was killed in the evening	

Army Form C. 2118.

WAR DIARY
or
INTELLIGENCE SUMMARY.
(Erase heading not required.)

Instructions regarding War Diaries and Intelligence Summaries are contained in F. S. Regs., Part II. and the Staff Manual respectively. Title pages will be prepared in manuscript.

Place	Date	Hour	Summary of Events and Information	Remarks and references to Appendices
MILLENCOURT	14/10/18		Reorganisation of Coys. — Training — Outposts: advance guards. Selected training — Range in afternoon.	
	15/10/18		Training — Range — Field firing etc. Brigadier inspected transport.	
	16/10/18		Training — Range — Coy in attack on/outposts.	
	17/10/18		Training — Range — Box Scheme.	
	18/10/18		Training — Range — Brigade Scheme.	
	19/10/18		Bn. moved a.m. according to Instructions attached from Bn. — all mounted officers and Buglers on horses and several tactical schemes were carried out.	
TROISVILLES	20/10/18		Lt Col. A. F. Lee D.S.O. assumed command vice Lt Col. Richie DSO took over 1st Queens Regt from him. 2Lt. Col Hon A Ritchie DSO rejoined + resumed command.	
	21/10/18		2Lts Johnson + Harlington at Bn.	

WAR DIARY
INTELLIGENCE SUMMARY

Army Form C. 2118.

Place	Date	Hour	Summary of Events and Information	Remarks and references to Appendices
TROISVILLES	22/10/18		Battn moved forward to assembly positions across SELLE River, east of SOLESMES-LE CATEAU Railway, in order to attack objective shown on map. 54 S.W. attached	
N of I/C	23/10/18		A, B & C Coys attacked at 2 am with D in reserve. The Battn reached the northern edge of VERDIGNY WOOD in front of its next objective. [illegible] were taken up.	
F 15 a.a	24/10/18		The 00Th Bde was then detailed to keep through our first K resisting line of [illegible] F.A.-Fna but no [illegible] were made to get on. The 10th Bde again attacked in the morning. The Battn attacked at Road Sq 8 - S 20 6. The Bn passed through it 6 S, 60 R, who had taken [illegible] at a 00.00 and succeeded in gaining the line of LITTLE FONTAINE - ORSINVAL RD. with D Coy in support about the TUILERIES--X During the night of 24/25/18 October our position was heavily shelled, a huge proportion of Gas Shells. Seeing our front ("EXIT FONTAINE" being occupied the attempt of work till towards morning, the idea of the Bde consisting in [illegible] of [illegible] road)	

WAR DIARY
or
INTELLIGENCE SUMMARY.

(Erase heading not required.)

Army Form C. 2118.

Place	Date	Hour	Summary of Events and Information	Remarks and references to Appendices
LES TILLEULS	28/8/18		The Bn. was concentrated at LES TILLEULS when formed into a defended locality held by Bn. during operations carried recorded in the capture of EWCR FONTAINE. The following casualties were incurred during these operations:- Killed: Lt. A.J. Bryatt. 2Lt. J.G. Cathro. 27 O.R. Wounded: Lt. Col. Hon. L. D.O. 2Lt. R.G. West. 2Lt. N.C. Dotson. 2Lt. R. Metcalf. 2Lt. B. Pennell. 169 O.R. Missing:- 6 O.R. Captures:- about 30 prisoners 1 Field gun 6 M.G.	

Army Form C. 2118.

WAR DIARY
or
INTELLIGENCE SUMMARY.
(Erase heading not required.)

Instructions regarding War Diaries and Intelligence Summaries are contained in F. S. Regs., Part II. and the Staff Manual respectively. Title pages will be prepared in manuscript.

Place	Date	Hour	Summary of Events and Information	Remarks and references to Appendices
TROISVILLES	26/10/18		On night of 26th inst. Bnanns was relieved by 38th Divn. Batt. returned to Billets in TROISVILLES.	
	27/10/18		Major J. Kirkwood M.C. resumed command of Bn. Reorganisation - cleaning up carried out.	
	28/10/18		Instructor to Corps Commander who congratulated all Bn. of Bde. on work done. Men marched to Baths at BERTRY.	
	29/10/18		Training. Special Classes for L.G. teams, Rifle Bombers. Range - platoons in attack - Employment of Lewis Gun.	
	30/10/18		Training — as above.	
	31/10/18			

John Kirkwood
Major
1st Bn.
Cmdg 1st Bn Cameronians

WAR DIARY

INTELLIGENCE SUMMARY

Army Form C. 2118

SECRET

19/33

Baw.Coucaus
(Pioneer Rifles)
Vol 5-2

Place	Date Nov. 1918	Hour	Summary of Events and Information	Remarks and references to Appendices
TROISVILLES	1		Rests in billets. Company training.	
	2			
	3	Sun.	Church parade.	
ENGLEFONTAIN	4		19th Brigade marches to ENGLEFONTAIN. Bn moved to M.10.c and arrived at dusk. Billeted in houses. No shelter for enemy having carried rest by to stack of 25th Div. is unruly.	
FORET de MORMAL	5		Advance through MORMAL FOREST. The 98th & 100th Bdes. led the way and by night were established on a line just West of the SAMBRE. 19th Bde. moved in columns of units by the Route d'Hecq, finally bivouacking in the night in the forest, 1 mile W. of SABARAS.	
	6		Bn began at 10 a.m. and continued all day a mid the 98th & 100th Bdes. crossed the SAMBRE during the night and established themselves well Est of the Sdo. At 10 a.m. the 19th Bde. began to move forward. The Bn. moved through SABARAS & SASSEGNIES and to SAMBREH & foot bridge in C.3.c. 1 mile South of BERLAIMONT, then proceeded in Artillery formation south of the railway and also moved through Pt 3/Wovecleau to PETIT MADERESE into the line of the	

H8 N
6 sheets

Army Form C. 2118.

WAR DIARY
or
INTELLIGENCE SUMMARY.
(Erase heading not required.)

Instructions regarding War Diaries and Intelligence Summaries are contained in F. S. Regs., Part II. and the Staff Manual respectively. Title pages will be prepared in manuscript.

Place	Date	Hour	Summary of Events and Information	Remarks and references to Appendices
PETIT MAUBEUGE	Nov 6 (con)	9/18	Chaussé BRUNEHAUT; 1500 yds to the East. Operation slight. Rain continued all day. Battalion with the 58th Div. on R. and 1/Queen's on L.	
POT de VIN	7		19F Bde. ordered to advance at dawn. Line East through POT de VIN. Final objective MAUBEUGE — AVESNES road in W.1.a.7. The Battn. moved forward at 5.45 am in a thick mist. POT de VIN was reached without opposition. Advance was continued through the wood but was held up in the Eastern Edge by strong M.G. fire from rise in front of DOURLERS. After some delay the 4/K.R.R. came up & attacked DOURLERS. Battn. then pushed on along the edge of the wood, meeting some opposition from M.G.s. Bn. ordered to dig in. D. Coy. were established on its final objective with other Coys. close behind. The [position] was somewhat precarious as the troops on left had not got beyond ECOUIN Dummy the night. 385/Div. came up to continue the advance.	

Army Form C. 2118.

WAR DIARY
or
INTELLIGENCE SUMMARY.
(Erase heading not required.)

Instructions regarding War Diaries and Intelligence Summaries are contained in F. S. Regs., Part II. and the Staff Manual respectively. Title pages will be prepared in manuscript.

Place	Date Nov. 1918	Hour	Summary of Events and Information	Remarks and references to Appendices
SABARAS	8		Batt. with drew in enemy and marched back to SABARAS. Total casualties 22. 4 killed, 7 missing, 11 wounded.	
"	9		to billets, cleaning up etc. General delegates in Paris, arrive to announce proposals to be given by Nov. 11th. V Corps to share in present British fighting armies.	
"	10	Sun	Church Parade.	
"	11		Inspection of Coys by C.O. Draft of 2 officers & 143 o.r. ranks arrived. Armistice signed by 11 A.M. Batt. marched to LIVET in BERLAIMONT.	
BERLAIMONT	12			
"	13			
"	14		Remained in billets, cleaning up.	
LOCQUIGNOL	15		The Bn. marched to LOCQUIGNOL, about 6 miles. Billets very bad. Troops crowded in anywhere. Band serenaded, played in first time.	

Army Form C. 2118.

WAR DIARY
or
INTELLIGENCE SUMMARY.
(Erase heading not required.)

Instructions regarding War Diaries and Intelligence Summaries are contained in F. S. Regs., Part II. and the Staff Manual respectively. Title pages will be prepared in manuscript.

Place	Date Nov. 1918	Hour	Summary of Events and Information	Remarks and references to Appendices
CROIX	16		The Bde. marched to CROIX about 8 miles. Weather bitterly cold and village much knocked about by shell fire.	
CLARY	17 Sun.		Bde. marched to CLARY about 10 miles. 9/G in at 1.30 p.m. 105th Bde. also billeted in the village. Draft of 2 Officers & 103 men joined the battn. north from 3rd Battn. 2/Lt. C.W. WOODS tried by Court Martial under A.A. Sec. 40. was sentenced to be Dismissed the Service. He was handed over to A.P.M. 33rd Divn.	
"	18		Cleaning up & inspection	
"	19		Drill. The Brigadier General inspected billets.	
"	20 to 23		P.T., drill and ceremonial parade	
"	24 Sun.		Church parade - Church Giving service to celebrate termination of the war.	
"	25		Battn. employed in collecting salvage between CLARY and BERTRY.	
"	26.		Brigade route march.	
"	27		Parades as usual	
"	28		Brigadier inspected transport.	

Army Form C. 2118.

WAR DIARY
or
INTELLIGENCE SUMMARY.
(Erase heading not required.)

Instructions regarding War Diaries and Intelligence Summaries are contained in F. S. Regs., Part II. and the Staff Manual respectively. Title pages will be prepared in manuscript.

Place	Date	Hour	Summary of Events and Information	Remarks and references to Appendices
CLARY	Nov 29 1918	-	Sixty miners left 11th Batt. to work in Scottish mines.	
"	30	-	Twenty miners left to work in mines.	

K.C. Hunter Lt.Col.
1/c Cameronians
Comdg.

Army Form C. 2118.

1 Scottish Rifles

26/12/5/2

WAR DIARY
or
INTELLIGENCE SUMMARY.
(Erase heading not required.)

Place	Date Dec. 1918	Hour	Summary of Events and Information	Remarks and references to Appendices
CLARY	1	Sun	Church parade.	
"	2		Brigade ceremonial parade, marching past etc.	
"	3		Brigade route march	
"	4		H.M. The King accompanied by the Prince of Wales passed through the village. Troops lined the streets.	
"	5		Training as usual.	
"	6		Inspection of transport by O.C. train	
"	7		Dull. PT musketry etc.	
"	8	Sun	Church parade.	
"	9-10		Training in billets owing to rain	
MASNIERES	11		The Division started to march to HORNOY Area. Battn. paraded at 9.15 A.M. and marched to MASNIERES about 8 miles. Billets fairly good, weather bad.	
HERMIES	12		Battn. marched to HERMIES about 10 miles. A very muddy camp, weather vile.	
FAVREUIL	13		marched to FAVREUIL about 11 miles, country devastated, billets in a line in SLL.	
ALBERT	14		marched to ALBERT, lay in a camp just west of the town.	

WAR DIARY or INTELLIGENCE SUMMARY

Army Form C. 2118.

Place	Date	Hour	Summary of Events and Information	Remarks and references to Appendices
PONT NOYELLES	Dec. 15.	Sun.	Marched to PONT NOYELLES about 12 miles. Billeted in Armstrong Huts.	
AILLY	16		Marched through Amiens to AILLY about 15 miles. Fair billets.	
LINCHEUX	17		C & D coys. to GOUY-L'HÔPITAL. Marched to LINCHEUX about 12 miles.	
"	18		⎫ Cleaning up and improvements to billets	
"	19		⎬	
"	20		⎭	
"	21		Kit inspection and drill parades	
"	22	Sun.	Church parades	
"	23		⎫ Wet weather made it impossible to hold any parades	
"	24		⎭	
"	25		Christmas Day	
"	26		⎫ Parades by companies. Education and Lewis Gun classes continued.	
"	27		⎬	
"	28		⎭ The Brigadier inspected the transport, which was very well turned out.	
"	29	Sun.	Church parades	
"	30		⎫ Parades by companies, to battalion hut huts at CAMPS.	
"	31		⎭	

1-1-19

Lt Col
Comdg 1st Cameronians

WAR DIARY or INTELLIGENCE SUMMARY

Army Form C. 2118

Place	Date 1919	Hour	Summary of Events and Information	Remarks and references to Appendices
LINCHEUX	Jan 1		Company runs. Bn. Rltn. beat 1st Queen's at football.	

"	2		Maj. Genl. Sir R. Pinney C.M.G. 33rd Divn. presented medal ribbons to the u/mentioned officers and men of the Battalion.
			Bar to M.C. Capt. F.C. Gobb M.C.
			M.C. 2/Lt. J. Stalton
			Mily. Medal Cpl. G. Ronald ⎫
			              4Cpl. S. Gorman ⎬ A
			              Pte M. Boyle ⎭
			              Pte M. Jones ⎫
			              4c. G. Bailey ⎬ B
			              Pte F. Duffie ⎭
			
			Mily. Medal Sgt. F. Brown ⎫
			              Pte. W. Brown ⎬ C
			              Pte W. Paul ⎭
			              C.S.M. Kinge ⎫
			              Cpl. W. Worgan ⎬ D
			              L/c. W. Moffat ⎬
			              Pte W. Aird ⎭	

"	3		Training in huts, owing to bad weather	
"	4		Battn. route march – Rte Lincheux – Hornoy – Gouy.	
"	5	Sun	Church Parades	
"	6		Educational & other Classes as heretofore.	

Army Form C. 2118.

WAR DIARY
or
INTELLIGENCE SUMMARY
(Erase heading not required)

Instructions regarding War Diaries and Intelligence Summaries are contained in F.S. Regs., Part II. and the Staff Manual respectively. Title pages will be prepared in manuscript.

Place	Date 1919 July	Hour	Summary of Events and Information	Remarks and references to Appendices
LINCHEUX	7		Educational classes, P.T. and one hours steady drill.	
"	8		As above. Football match Officers v. Sergts.	
"	9		As above.	
"	10		As above. Football match versus Pole 1.9	
"	11		Warn to move to ROUEN received.	
"	12		45 men left the battalion, warned to proceed to Demobilization Centre in England. A few regular soldiers with unexpired colour service to do P.G. heavy all Tent 45 men the hue with the Battn through the Great Cart of the war. The G.Ws for hor-12 strain including Pipes Reed had Jamsly. Other old soldiers were Sgt Hanley Saunders Sgt C.H.C. Webb Fisher CoM Gordon Piper	
"	13		The Battn paraded at 6.30 a.m. and marched to POIX when it entrained, unto the 5th Scot Rifles & T.M.B. The Queen's had left the line about a week previously.	

Army Form C. 2118.

WAR DIARY
or
INTELLIGENCE SUMMARY.
(Erase heading not required.)

Instructions regarding War Diaries and Intelligence Summaries are contained in F.S. Regs., Part II. and the Staff Manual respectively. Title pages will be prepared in manuscript.

Place	Date 1919 July	Hour	Summary of Events and Information	Remarks and references to Appendices
ROUEN	14	Tues	The Battn. arrived at ROUEN after dark 13th and marched at 15:15 to Medical Board Camp. Officers in huts, men in tents with beds for them. Normans.	
"	15		Company parades and fatigue parties.	
"	16		Battalion parade, ceremonial drill. Football match in afternoon.	
"	17		Transport which left LONGUENEUX on 13:15 and travelled by road arrived. Stabled at No 6 Vety. Hosp. about 1 mile from Camp.	
"	18		Company hut inspection.	
"	19	Sun	Church parades.	
"	20		Found guards in six different camps, 114 men being employed.	
"	21		10 men left on demobilization.	
"	22		The whole Battalion was employed on Guards and fatigues.	
"	23		10 men left on demobilization. Pipe Major Alexander & Pte Dymoley (transport) awarded M.S.M.	

Army Form C. 2118.

WAR DIARY
or
INTELLIGENCE SUMMARY.
(Erase heading not required.)

Instructions regarding War Diaries and Intelligence Summaries are contained in F.S. Regs., Part II. and the Staff Manual respectively. Title pages will be prepared in manuscript.

Place	Date 1919	Hour	Summary of Events and Information	Remarks and references to Appendices
ROUEN	24		Greater part of the Battn. on Guard over Prisoners camp etc. (Demand is steadily continues at the rate of 10 men a day)	
"	25			
"	26	Sun	Church parade	
"	27		Guards and fatigues	
"	28		Concert given by French officers to the British in Barrie Hall Rouen. Pipers performed in the interval. Very wet weather set in.	
"	29		Practically every man on Guard. (Demobilization proceeding on lines then still going away at rate of 10 a day. Strength of battn. now 425.	
"	30			
"	31		Got another hut from R.E., thus enabling all men to be in huts.	
	31-1-19			[Signed] C.H. Smith Lt Col. Comdg. the Cameronians

1/7 Scots
1 Scottish Rifles
of 1/9th The Camerons & others
9/2/57

51.11
3 sheets

WAR DIARY
INTELLIGENCE SUMMARY

Place	Date	Hour	Summary of Events and Information	Remarks and references to Appendices
ROUEN 1919	Feby 1		Demobilisation proceeding at rate of 10 men a day.	
"	2	Sun	Church parades	
"	3		Half of the Battalion on Guard. Beat the 5/Sco Rifles at Football.	
"	4		Guards etc	
"	5		The Band, 37 or so under Mr Dowell arrived from home.	
"	6		Heavy fall of snow during the night. First plentiful.	
"	7		Very cold, hard frost. Guards as usual.	
"	8			
"	9	Sun	Church parades	
"	10		Demobilisation proceeded during the past week at rate of 10 men per day	
"	11		That of the Battalion on Guards & fatigues	
"	12		Snow lying, frost continued.	
"	13			
"	14		A draft arrived from the 2nd Battalion, consisting of 6 officers & 132 men. These are all men in the army of tempr. service.	

Army Form C. 2118.

WAR DIARY
or
INTELLIGENCE SUMMARY.
(Erase heading not required.)

Instructions regarding War Diaries and Intelligence Summaries are contained in F. S. Regs., Part II. and the Staff Manual respectively. Title pages will be prepared in manuscript.

Place	Date 1919 Feby	Hour	Summary of Events and Information	Remarks and references to Appendices
ROUEN	15	Saty	The Battn. gave a concert in the Y.M.C.A. to entertain the residents of the Road	
			Amiens and Officers and men attended.	
	16	Sun	Church parades	
	17		50 men on guard. The remainder on fatigues, etc	
	18		Route for the Battn. at White House.	
	19		Band of the Royal Engineers played in the Y.M.C.A. hut.	
	20		Guards etc as usual. a wet day	
	21	}	Guards & fatigues	
	22	}		
	23	Sun	Church parades	
	24		Strikes and demn. for N.C.O.'s under the R.S.M.	
	25		Guards & fatigues as usual. Practically all returnable men have now gone away, leaving only the cadre men (or army of occupation.	
	26		The Battalion gave a concert in the Y.M.C.A., the band being assisted by various artistes.	

Army Form C. 2118.

WAR DIARY
or
INTELLIGENCE SUMMARY.
(Erase heading not required.)

Instructions regarding War Diaries and Intelligence Summaries are contained in F. S. Regs., Part II. and the Staff Manual respectively. Title pages will be prepared in manuscript.

Place	Date Feby	Hour	Summary of Events and Information	Remarks and references to Appendices
ROUEN	27		Guards & fatigues as usual day.	
	28		Guards at F.P. Camp — 58 General Hospital — 10 General Hospital.	
			28-2-19	A.E. White, Lt. Col. Cmdg. The Garrison.

WAR DIARY
of 1st Bn. Cameronians (Scottish Rifles)
INTELLIGENCE SUMMARY
(Erase heading not required.)

Place	Date	Hour	Summary of Events and Information
ROUEN 1919	1 March		Water tanks off in camp for two days. Water carts going day & night to fetch water.
"	2	Sun	Church parade.
"	3		Wet day. Band played in the Y.M.C.A. in afternoon.
"	4		Company parades. C.Q.M.S. Hotley & Sgt Kinnell granted the Mily. Medal.
"	5		Brig. Genl. Mayne Cmdg. 19th Inf. Bde. inspected the Battn in parade.
"	6		16 officers & 282 men were on parade. Battalion Route march for 1½ hrs. Men went into Camp.
"	7		The Brigadier General Commanding sent the folly. message to the battalion:— "The G.O.C. wishes to express his satisfaction at the smart turnout and soldier like bearing of the Cameronians on the recent inspection parade and route march. The equipment was clean & well put on and the steadiness in the ranks and handling of arms were excellent. In view of the shortage of rain and so frequent N.C.O's Yest. credit is due to all ranks for turn out & parade."

52. 11
4 sheets

Army Form C. 2118.

WAR DIARY
or
INTELLIGENCE SUMMARY.
(Erase heading not required.)

Instructions regarding War Diaries and Intelligence Summaries are contained in F. S. Regs., Part II. and the Staff Manual respectively. Title pages will be prepared in manuscript.

Place	Date 1919 March	Hour	Summary of Events and Information	Remarks and references to Appendices
ROUEN	8 Sat.		Parades & fatigues as usual.	
	9 Sun.		All men went to White House for baths and clean clothing.	
	10		⎫ Practically all men on Guards or working parties	
	11		⎬	
	12		⎭ The Batt. played the R. Ordnance Corps in the Armistice Cup. Score — Cameroons 6 goals — Ordnance 3 goals	
	13		Guards & Fatigues.	
	14		Regimental concert in the Recp[tion] Camp Y.M.C.A.	
	15		Guards & Fatigues.	
	16 Sun		Church Parades.	
	17		Practically all men on Guards.	
	18		Inspection of Guards by O.C. Rouen garrison. A number of Z's were taken in sick and then carried on to this place.	

D. D. & L., London, E.C.
(A6001) Wt. W1771/M2931 750,000 5/17 **Sch. 52** Forms/C2118/14

Army Form C. 2118.

WAR DIARY
or
INTELLIGENCE SUMMARY.
(Erase heading not required.)

Instructions regarding War Diaries and Intelligence Summaries are contained in F. S. Regs., Part II. and the Staff Manual respectively. Title pages will be prepared in manuscript.

Place	Date	Hour	Summary of Events and Information	Remarks and references to Appendices
ROUEN	1919 March 19th		Brigadier General inspected Remnants of Thirsk Details. the Battn. Lieut Camidien 32nd Echelon in Khaki to take Communion. 3 goals Canadian 1 goal. 1st 1 game was played at 9t Etienne.	
	20th		Practically all men on leave	
	21st		Slight distrubance in N⁰ 6 Hut. many of a B.W.I. patient upstairs went to a party of 40 men went and attacked & other patients in hut.	
	22nd			
	23rd Sun		Church parades	
	24th Mon		All men on leave or fatigues	
	25th			
	26th		A draft of 6 Upper + 179 men arrived from T⁰ 12th H.L.I. 35th Division. These men were divided equally between Companies.	

Army Form C. 2118.

WAR DIARY
or
INTELLIGENCE SUMMARY.
(Erase heading not required.)

Instructions regarding War Diaries and Intelligence Summaries are contained in F. S. Regs., Part II. and the Staff Manual respectively. Title pages will be prepared in manuscript.

Place	Date 1919 March	Hour	Summary of Events and Information	Remarks and references to Appendices
Rouen	27		A wet day to my day. The Brigadier inspected draft for H.L.I. Played the R.A.S.C. on the Rouen Ground in the semi-final of the Armistice Cup. Our team were out-played and never had a chance of winning. Saw R.A.S.C. 6 goals — Camerons Nil.	
"	28		All the men draft in the square to learn Rifle drill.	
"	29		Notification received that 10th Battn. will need trainers.	
"	30	Sun	10th Battn. arrived about 11 a.m. 9 officers & 200 men Commanded by Lt Col. Foulis D.S.O.	
"	31		Three battalion returned to Calais, at surplus officers & O.R.'s were being posted to 10th Scottish Rifles from this draft.	

F.C. Holmitt. Lt Col
Comdg. 1th Camerons
31-3-19

1 Scottish Rifles

M 56

53.M.
2 sheets

WAR DIARY
or
INTELLIGENCE SUMMARY

Army Form C. 2118.

Place	Date	Hour	Summary of Events and Information	Remarks and references to Appendices
	April 1919		The Cadre of the Battalion remained at ROUEN in a Camp adjacent to that occupied by 10th Battalion Scottish Rifles. A cement was given weekly. On April 20th - a football match consisting of a mixed team from the Cadre and 10th Battalion Scottish Rifles played the remainder of ROUEN.	

Army Form C. 2118.

WAR DIARY
or
INTELLIGENCE SUMMARY.

(Erase heading not required.)

Instructions regarding War Diaries and Intelligence
Summaries are contained in F. S. Regs., Part II.
and the Staff Manual respectively. Title pages
will be prepared in manuscript.

Place	Date	Hour	Summary of Events and Information	Remarks and references to Appendices
April			Resulting in a drawn game.	

H.C. Wait
Lt. Colonel
Commdg. the Cameronians

ORDERLY ROOM
No...........
2 MAY 1919
1st BATTALION
THE CAMERONIANS
(SCOTTISH RIFLES)

WAR DIARY
or
INTELLIGENCE SUMMARY.
(Erase heading not required.)

Army Form ___
1 Scottish ___
98 67

Place	Date	Hour	Summary of Events and Information	Remarks and references to Appendices
ROUEN.	1.5.19		A concert was given by the Battalion in Y.M.C.A. All ranks were forbidden to enter ROUEN on account of threatened riots by the French Population.	
"	2.5.19		Lieut-Col. H.C.H. Smith, D.S.O. was admitted to No. 6 General Hospital. Capt. C.R. Wigan, M.C. assumed command of the Battalion.	
"	4.5.19		ROUEN Mounted Sports meeting held at BIHOREL Race Course. The band played during the afternoon and evening. The Commanding Officer's charger won an event.	
"	9.5.19		The Cadre was inspected by Lieut-Col. H.B. Spens, D.S.O. Commanding the 19th Inf. Brigade.	
"	15.5.19		Capt. C.R. Wigan, M.C. proceeded to England to take up duties at the War Office, and was struck strength of Battalion. Capt. H.G. Galbraith assumed command.	

WAR DIARY
or
INTELLIGENCE SUMMARY.
(Erase heading not required.)

Instructions regarding War Diaries and Intelligence Summaries are contained in F. S. Regs., Part II. and the Staff Manual respectively. Title pages will be prepared in manuscript.

Place	Date	Hour	Summary of Events and Information	Remarks and references to Appendices
ROUEN	16.5.19		Lieut Col. W.C.H. Smith, D.S.O. posted to 10th Scottish Rifles and struck of strength of Cadre.	
"	23.5.19		The Cadre in conjunction with the 10th Scottish Rifles held sports. The Band played during the afternoon and evening.	
"	24.5.19		Major J. Kirkwood, M.C. rejoined the Cadre from No. I. Staging Camp, BUSHEY, and assumed command.	

John Kirkwood
Major
Commanding 1st The Cameronians
(Sco. Rifles).

ORDERLY ROOM
No. Ad 417
5 [ ] 1919
1ST BATTALION
THE CAMERONIANS
(SCOTTISH RIFLES)

www.ingramcontent.com/pod-product-compliance
Lightning Source LLC
Chambersburg PA
CBHW080918230426
43668CB00014B/2153